A Penitent People

THE DOCTRINE OF REPENTANCE

Harrison Perkins

Unless otherwise noted, all emphasis in Scripture has been added by the author.

print ISBN 978-1-5271-1255-1

ebook ISBN 978-1-5271-1387-9

10 9 8 7 6 5 4 3 2 1

Published in 2025
by
Christian Focus Publications Ltd.,
Geanies House, Fearn, Ross-shire
IV20 1TW, Great Britain.

www.christianfocus.com

Cover design by Rubner Durais
Internal artwork by Sarah Perkins

Printed and bound by
Bell and Bain Glasgow

Repentance, both in theory and practice, is sadly neglected today. Perkins' book is a wonderful tonic for that neglect, showing not simply the necessity and duty of repentance, but its gracious source in the ongoing ministry of the Lord Jesus. True gospel repentance is not something we work up in ourselves to earn the right to God's favour, rather it is the gift of Jesus Himself, who "God exalted to his own right hand as Prince and Saviour that he might bring Israel to repentance and forgive their sins" (Acts 5:31). As Perkins shows, this perspective transforms repentance from a negative burden to "a joyful and happy endeavour in the Christian life." May this book be used to lead many to true gospel repentance!

Donald John MacLean

President, Westminster Seminary, UK

Although the manna in the wilderness was extraordinary in its origin, it was ordinary in its occurrence. It was a regular part of Israel's rhythm of life, just as it was essential to that life. So also, repentance is "an ordinary part of the Christian life." Supernatural in its origin, "repentance unto life" is designed to be a regular, yet vital grace in our walk with Christ. In *A Penitent People*, Perkins alerts us to the danger of mistaking a routine practice for an inferior one. He identifies views and habits that are not true friends of repentance, while he highlights those that are more worthy company of its good name. Here, "godly sorrow" is presented in its health and beauty, and it will particularly comfort those whose sorrow is never sorrowful enough. In all this discussion, the sufficient grace of God in Christ is ever present—as it is in the ministries of all good Marrowmen.

A. Craig Troxel

Professor of Practical Theology, Westminster Seminary, Escondido, California

This isn't just another book about sin and sorrow—it's a heartfelt invitation to see repentance as the joyful rhythm of the Christian life, grounded in the unwavering grace of Christ. Perkins deftly weaves Scripture, the Reformed tradition, and practical wisdom to remind us that Christian repentance isn't a burdensome duty but a liberating joy. Whether you're a bruised soul needing assurance or a stubborn one needing a nudge, this book will point you to Jesus—the only Savior who frees us from sin's penalty and its power. Read it, repent, and rejoice.

Patrick Abendroth
Pastor, Omaha Bible Church, Omaha, Nebraska

Repentance: a grace-wrought turning from sin to God and one of the benefits of our faith that is often overlooked in the Christian life. Dr. Perkins takes us on a journey that starts with the awesomeness of faith, recognizes the consequences of sin, but rejoices in the sanctifying freedom that true repentance can bring to the Christian life. If repentance is often considered something that is simply part of our conversion, then this book helps us to locate it as part of genuine revival and the beauty of God's sanctifying work in our life. I will be recommending this book often to my brothers and sisters who are serious about their personal and corporate spiritual formation. *A Penitent People* helps us to understand how this vital work of the Holy Spirit leads to forgiveness, reconciliation, and a life lived in thankful submission to God's sovereign will.

Ike Reeder
President, Birmingham Theological Seminary,
Birmingham, Alabama

In memory of

Rev. Dr. Harry L. Reeder III
(1948–2023)

Forever and always my pastor.

CONTENTS

INTRODUCTION

Repentance is about Christ freeing His people from sin's enslaving power. It is about increasingly knowing reprieve from sin's grip and tyranny as we mature in the Christian life. It concerns release from that which damages our relationship with God and with one another. This book, therefore, aims to explore various facets of repentance to help us come to value it as a blessed feature of the Christian life.

Because sin does damage to our relationship with God individually and to our relationships with one another, repentance is relevant at the level of individuals and of the church community. In other words, each one of us personally needs to be repentant, and our church community holistically needs to be repentant. The individual and the corporate sense of repentance are both necessary. These two layers of relevance inform how this book develops its case.

As the book progresses, our reflections on repentance will move from focusing on individual repentance to focus on why our church community should be characterized by repentance. The reason for moving from individual to corporate considerations about repentance concerns keeping a balanced perspective about how to emphasize repentance. On the one hand, modern western culture has an impulse to locate sin within systemic problems. Although that outlook has fitting application to some issues, our initial focus on the need for individual repentance helps Christians to take personal responsibility for their sin without placing the blame entirely upon external structures. Every person is a sinner who needs to repent. On the other hand, a community composed of individuals who are repentant should grow in its collective outlook of repentance so that a posture of repentance paints the whole group. Repentance should be something that also develops as an ethos among Christ's people. To keep these perspectives in balance, this book tackles both by developing its argument, beginning with the individual aspects, and then shifting to the corporate dimensions.

Thanks to several people who read and provided invaluable feedback on earlier drafts (in order of their feedback's appearance): Jonathan Cruse, R. Scott Clark, J. V. Fesko, Craig Troxel, Olan Stubbs, and David Strain. Thanks also to the team at Christian Focus, and especially Colin Fast, for bringing this project to life. Throughout my experience in pastoral ministry, repentance has been an issue that I have recognized as a challenge for Christians. I am grateful for the opportunity to express in print my pastoral burden for this issue with hopes to help a wider audience of Christians appreciate the riches of repentance.

Thanks finally to the many personal connections who have given inestimable support to this work. The congregation of Oakland Hills Community Church (OPC) is an amazing community of believers, and I am so grateful to be their pastor. Their encouragement and love are of such ongoing help to me even as I strive to be a help to them. The Lord has been kind to let me be their pastor. Thanks to the elders at OHCC for the ways that they practically support me to keep writing as a way to (I hope!) bless our congregation and the wider church. Thanks to my dear family, Sarah and Scott, for bearing with a sinful husband and father who often has to repent. You both are more of a blessing than I ever could deserve, but are the exact blessing that I need.

As I dedicate this volume to Harry Reeder, words escape me for how to express my appreciation for him and why I would try to honor his memory with this book. Harry was my pastor from 2008, when I joined Briarwood Presbyterian Church, until I was ordained in 2017 by the Evangel Presbytery, where Harry was also a Presbyter. He was a continual source of wisdom and kindness to me as I learned about Reformed theology, as I progressed toward ministry, and as I have grown as a pastor. Not a single week has gone by since his (from a human perspective) sudden and untimely death that I have not thought about him and missed his presence in my life. Before his passing, it often felt like I was merely pretending in pastoral ministry while the giants like him were doing it for real. I know how he would laugh at me for voicing that sentiment. Yet, whatever usefulness I might have for Christ's church, I know, at least in part, it owes to the mark that Harry has left on my life. Inasmuch as this book aims to point God's people to the riches of what Christ can do in your life, it seems the most fitting tribute to Harry that I am able to produce. He certainly did that for me.

Chapter One

THE BLESSING OF REPENTANCE

Sin makes us miserable. It ruins our present lives and, if we do not find salvation in Christ, it will—to put it mildly—ruin our lives for eternity as well. Sin's toll is high, casting long shadows over our whole existence. Sin wreaks havoc upon every fiber of our being and corrupts us to the core. We do our best to pretend that we are fine, but, at the end of the day, we all know that our sin has left us wanting.

Sin's bleak effects serve to spotlight this book's fundamental argument that repentance is a joyful aspect of the Christian life. Our focus is not on that hard fallout that comes from sin and its misery but on the beautiful freedom that comes from Christ in turning us away from sin. The Christian life is supposed to be a life of freedom, ever increasing freedom from sin's curse. Christ came and has provided deliverance for His people.

Spectacularly, Jesus provides freedom from both sin's penalty *and* power. Christ is our comprehensive Savior. This book is about how adopting the posture and practice of repentance is a key way to increasingly enjoy that freedom from sin's power. Hence, we might sing:

Kind and merciful God,
In Christ's death on the cross you provided cleansing from sin;
Speak the words that forgive
That henceforth we may live
by the might of your Spirit within.[1]

This hymn provides some perspective on how we might distinguish sin's *ruling* power and its power of *influence*. Christ has broken its *rule* over our lives so that we no longer *have to* sin (Rom. 6:15-23). Westminster Confession of Faith 16.3 explains that believers' "ability to do good works is not at all of themselves, but wholly from the Spirit of Christ," and further, "that they may be enabled thereunto, beside the grace that have already received, there is required an actual influence of the same Holy Spirit, to work in them to will, and to do, of his good pleasure" (Phil. 2:13). By the Spirit's influence, those who have already been saved by Christ can proceed to do imperfect but truly good works, which serve as "the fruits and evidences of a lively faith."[2] God, in His saving power, enables us to choose righteousness instead of sin. Nevertheless, sin also still exercises influence over us in all that we do. We are tempted and, in our fallenness, find sin appealing and enticing. In this respect, although God has broken sin's ruling power, repentance is a fight against sin's power of influence.[3]

---

1 Bryan Jeffery Leech, "Kind and Merciful God, We Have Sinned," in *Trinity Psalter Hymnal* (Trinity Psalter Hymnal Joint Venture, 2018), 180.

2 Westminster Confession of Faith 16.2.

3 Thanks to Olan Stubbs for helpful insight on this distinction.

Part of why we might not enjoy the freedom which Christ provides for us is that we adopt a lopsided view of His saving work, wherein He provides forgiveness and the Spirit's empowering. This sort of skewed perspective often happens when we reduce the benefits of Christ to one aspect of what He has done for us, in terms of providing rescue either from sin's penalty or power. How does a lopsided perspective occur? How do we avoid it?

The Pastoral Burden for Christ's Twofold Benefit

The Reformed tradition has long cherished the distinction of the *twofold benefit* of Christ. Heidelberg Catechism 70 highlights these dual blessings, asking, "What does it mean to be washed with Christ's blood *and* Spirit?" The answer first emphasizes how God pardons us in justification, as "To be washed with Christ's blood means to receive the forgiveness of sins from God, through grace, because of Christ's blood, poured out for us in his sacrifice on the cross." Further, God restores us as "To be washed with his Spirit means to be renewed by the Holy Spirit and sanctified to be members of Christ, so that more and more we become dead to sin and lead a holy and blameless life."[4] This double grace, or the twofold benefit, of Christ, helps us to see that God provides a new standing with Him as well as true renewal of our lives.

On the one hand, God *justifies* us, meaning that He declares us righteous in His sight both by forgiving our sin on account of Christ's death on our behalf and by counting us as fully righteous on account of Christ's perfect record

4 All references from the Westminster Standards and the Three Forms of Unity come from Peter A. Lillback and Bernard Aubert (eds.), *Reformed Standards of Unity: The Historic Statements of Faith Confessed by the Presbyterian and Reformed Churches* (Westminster Seminary Press, 2023). I have modernized verb tenses in many instances. Emphasis added.

of law-keeping. God justifies us by applying both these aspects of Christ's saving work to us. This benefit is a legal benefit wherein we receive a new status with God. We are made right with God and adopted into His family only on account of Christ's work for us, received by faith alone. In this respect, God saves sinners apart from any works on their part, since "to the one who does not work but believes in him who *justifies the ungodly,* his faith is counted as righteousness" (Rom. 4:5). God's free grace removes sin's *penalty* in justification before and apart from any personal renewal or works of new obedience in the believer.

On the other hand, as Westminster Shorter Catechism 35 explains, God *sanctifies* us, meaning that He works in us to enable us to die unto sin more and more, and to live unto Christ. Although He brings us into a new relationship with Him apart from any renewal in us, God does provide that renewal of our lives. He, as Calvin put it, cultivates true (albeit imperfect) blamelessness and purity of life in us. This benefit of sanctification is a renovative blessing wherein God works real change in us. He continues to work in us because "he who began a good work in you will bring it to completion at the day of Jesus Christ" (Phil. 1:6). God's free grace, therefore, also progressively removes sin's *power* in sanctification as He changes us to be increasingly like Christ our Redeemer. Christ, having broken sin's ruling power over us, also helps us fight its power of influence.

Lopsidedness comes when we fail to cherish these distinct benefits of Christ on their own terms for how they are blessings of God's grace, given to those whom God loves and rescues in Christ. We can fail to cherish these benefits in two ways that are relevant for our considerations about repentance. First, we might succeed in cherishing justification in such a way that, as it assures us of God's free grace so forcefully, we might not see how sanctification is also a *blessing* from Christ. It is a good thing to grow in grace, and Christians are called to do it! We should avoid the assumption that freedom from sin's penalty nullifies our need for freedom from sin's power. Second, we might so cherish sanctification and the freedom Christ gives us from sin's power that we make the grave error of making our justification dependent on our sanctification. We must also avoid the lopsided assumption that the blessing of freedom from sin's power controls whether we are free from sin's penalty. Justification and sanctification are distinct benefits of salvation. If we lack appreciation for this distinction, we will not properly emphasize that our renewed relationship with God in justification is neither founded nor contingent upon our renewed life of holiness in sanctification.

Sanctification will, of course, always be imperfect in this life. It may well be robust and rich. Nevertheless, it will never be complete until we go to glory. We must keep this point in mind as we consider repentance. As sanctification is partial and gradual in this life, so repentance, as an aspect of sanctification, will remain a struggle to some degree as well. Since our sanctification will not be perfect in this life, neither will our repentance. We must press ahead for continual growth in both. In this respect, we must also remember that sanctification is the dynamic benefit of Christ. Justification is stable and static, having no room to develop or grow. In the double benefit of Christ, sanctification is where we expect to see increase and development.

Repentance fits into this appreciation of Christ's double benefit in that it is a premiere feature of our sanctification. John Calvin rightly understood that repentance is a vital characteristic of the Christian life, so much so that he at times referred to the entirety of our sanctification as repentance. After explaining that repentance consists both of increasingly putting sin to death (mortification) and of increasingly practicing holiness (vivification), he explains both as aspects of the renewal that we receive in Christ: "Both things happen to us by participation in Christ ... Therefore, in a word, I interpret repentance as regeneration, whose sole end is to restore in us the image of God that had been disfigured and all but obliterated through Adam's transgression."[5] Importantly, both aspects of our renewal, our ongoing regeneration, are summed up as repentance wherein we are increasingly brought to reflect God's image (Eph. 4:24; Col. 3:10). Repentance is then the prevailing aspect of our life of sanctification, as we learn to be rid of sin and to know greater freedom in Christ.

Faith is a key consideration to help us cherish Christ's distinct benefits on their own terms. Those *who belong to Christ* receive repentance as an aspect of the blessing of sanctification. Inasmuch as we receive Christ by faith, repentance is a gift that comes to us from Christ through faith and union with Him. Reflecting upon God's promise to renew His people's hearts, John Colquhoun highlights God's wonderful provision of repentance as a gift: "As it is the office of the Mediator *to give repentance*, so he gives it to his elect by performing these promises to them: 'I will take away the stony heart out of your flesh, and I will give you an heart of flesh' (Ezek. 36:36)."[6] Thus, "faith of redeeming mercy is

---

5 John Calvin, *Institutes of the Christian Religion*, ed. John T. McNeil, trans. Ford Lewis Battles, 2 vols. (The Library of Christian Classics; Westminster John Knox Press, 1960), 3.3.9.

6 John Colquhoun, *Repentance* (The Banner of Truth Trust, 2010), 7.

a spring of true repentance."[7] Even as faith and repentance stand in the closest relation, we must not fail to see how true faith is the wellspring of true repentance:

> The exercise of evangelical repentance is one of the fruits, and therefore one of the evidences, of that faith which purifies the heart, and works by love. Although the principles of faith and the principle of repentance are in the moment of regeneration implanted in the soul together and at once, yet the exercise of faith in the order of nature, goes before the exercise of true repentance.[8]

God embeds the root of faith in our hearts to produce the bloom of repentance in our lives.

Faith is the fount of sanctification and, hence, the source of repentance. Calvin drives home the point again in relation to Christ's twofold benefit: "Now, both repentance and forgiveness of sins—that is, the newness of life and free reconciliation—are conferred on us by Christ, and both are attained by us through faith."[9] As he reflected upon this connection, Calvin also saw that the gospel offers us these blessings as free gifts of grace:

> For when this topic [repentance] is rightly understood it will better appear how man is justified by faith alone, and simple pardon; nevertheless actual holiness of life, so to speak, is not separated from free imputation of righteousness. Now, it ought to be a fact beyond controversy that repentance not only constantly follows faith, but is also born of faith.[10]

7 Colquhoun, *Repentance*, 14.

8 Colquhoun, *Repentance*, 61.

9 Calvin, *Institutes*, 3.3.1.

10 Calvin, *Institutes*, 3.3.1.

If we reflect upon Calvin's admonition to understand the gospel rightly, we will discover an important feature of hope that enables greater faithfulness in the Christian life.

Many of us learn to ride a bicycle by using training wheels. They hold our bike upright while we learn how to perform the motions of peddling and steering. What if we took the training wheel off one side though? That would be entirely unhelpful because the support on one side would continually push us to fall down on the other. Removing one training wheel creates a lopsidedness in how we can ride a bicycle. The same is true if we do not keep both sides of the double benefit of Christ firmly in place. Our practice of the Christian life will become lopsided in how we think about sin and our standing with God.[11]

The gospel, rightly understood, is God's promise of life in *every* respect. It should fill us with joy! Too often, Christians assume that the gospel *offers* forgiveness of sin but then *demands* new obedience. The better understanding, as we reflect with Calvin, is that the gospel offers forgiveness of sin *and also offers* new life of repentance and increasing obedience to God. Although new obedience is truly a *responsibility* for every Christian, it is a *blessing* offered to us in the gospel as a benefit from Christ. After reflecting upon the great truth of salvation by grace alone through faith alone apart from works, Paul applied this very reality: "For we are his workmanship, created in Christ Jesus for good works, which God prepared beforehand, that we should walk in them" (Eph. 2:10). God has done the work of saving us, giving us the gift of new life so that we can walk in good deeds of service to our Maker and Redeemer. Augustine (A.D. 354–430), the ancient church's foremost champion of grace, encapsulated how our renewed

11 Thanks to David Strain for this training wheels metaphor.

life and all our potential repentant deeds are gifts of God's grace to sinners: "And all my hope is nowhere except in your great mercy. Grant us what you command, and command us what you will."[12] In the gospel, God promises us new life, which He confers upon us in the double benefit of Christ by grace alone through faith alone, namely, justification and sanctification as gifts of His blessing.

This book was born out of a pastoral concern to avoid both forms of lopsidedness and to bring joy to our ongoing life of sanctification. More specifically, our purpose is to think together about how it is a great blessing from Christ that we can turn away from our sin. God's people should delight in their hearts to know that Christ grants freedom from sin in all its respects. He does not grant *full* freedom from sin's power until we meet Him in glory and are, as Westminster Shorter Catechism 37 says, "made perfect in holiness." Nevertheless, He grants us *true* freedom from sin in this life in all its respects by delivering us entirely from its penalty in justification and increasingly from its power in sanctification.

Repentance fits into this pastoral concern because it is arguably the foremost way wherein God's people might come to enjoy that increasing freedom from sin's power. Most Christians do not naturally associate the words "repentance" and "enjoy." Hence, the pastoral burden of this book. We should see repentance as freedom, as a blessing, and as a good thing. Indeed, not only as a good thing but as a *great* thing—a joyful and happy endeavor in the Christian life. We have a bad view of it when we see it as scary or a bleak necessity. Either of these mistaken outlooks reveals

12 Saint Augustine, *The Confessions of Saint Augustine*, trans. Rex Warner (Signet Classics, 1963), 10.29.

that we have adopted one of those lopsided views of Christ's twofold benefit.

How does repentance rightly help this pastoral concern? If we understand repentance rightly in relation to justification, in no way can it be scary. God has dealt with the penalty of our sin in justification, so that He has freely and forever forgiven and accepted everyone who has faith in Christ. If we understand repentance rightly as part of the ongoing life of sanctification, in no way can it be a bleak necessity. Repentance is a gift that God gives so that we turn away from what makes us miserable. Even with the full forgiveness of sin in justification, we can be experientially miserable when sin's power still makes its effects known in our lives. Hence, we should *enjoy* repentance as an act of turning away from that which inflicts misery.

Repentance in the Reformed Tradition

The Reformed confessions provide good material to guide our reflections throughout this book. They emphasize how repentance is a gift coming from God by grace. They emphasize how repentance is a staple feature of the Christian life that ought to increase over time as a matter of Spirit-fueled maturity. They emphasize that joy is the result of our repentance as we know greater experience of new life.

Westminster Shorter Catechism 87 most helpfully emphasizes God's work of grace in our repentance. It describes "repentance unto life" as "a saving grace, whereby a sinner, out of a true sense of his sin, and apprehension of the mercy of God in Christ, does, with grief and hatred of his sin, turn from it unto God, with full purpose of, and endeavor after, new obedience." The first part of the catechism's answer picks up important exegetical points from when Peter reported in Jerusalem about the Gentiles becoming Christians. After Peter's explanation of how God had directed him to reach out to the Gentiles, we have the account of Peter's experience with the Gentiles and his hearers' response in Acts 11:15-18:

> "As I began to speak, the Holy Spirit fell on them just as on us at the beginning. And I remembered the word of the Lord, how he said, 'John baptized with water, but you will be baptized with the Holy Spirit.' If then God gave the same gift to them as he gave to us when we believed in the Lord Jesus Christ, who was I that I could stand in God's way?" When they heard these things they fell silent. And they glorified God, saying, "Then to the Gentiles also God has granted repentance that leads to life."

This interaction contains more than might meet the eye about the nature of repentance. One clear point is that the Holy Spirit comes as God's gift to those who believed in Christ. The Spirit coming to the Gentiles is "the same gift" that the Jewish Christians received "*when* we believed in the Lord Jesus Christ." The acknowledgement of the reality that they had received the Spirit by faith led Peter's hearers to infer that God had given them the gift of repentance that leads to life.[13] John Colquhoun explains:

> Implanted by the Spirit at regeneration, it is so inseparably connected with salvation, as to constitute an essential part of it. In the Scriptures it is called, "repentance to salvation," and "repentance unto life" (Acts 11:18); as it proceeds from, and

13 See the Assembly's discussion on repentance in relation to faith and justification as recorded in Chad Van Dixhoorn (ed.), *John Lightfoot's Journals of the Westminster Assembly* (Oxford University Press, 2023), 90-93.

> evidences spiritual life in the soul, and as it prepares for, and issues in the perfection of life eternal.[14]

Repentance is a sign of spiritual life that is preparing us in this age for everlasting life.

We see now why the catechism says that "Repentance unto life is a saving grace." Repentance was in these Gentiles only because the Spirit had taken residence in them *when they believed* in Christ. As the Spirit indwells us by faith, He prompts us directly to turn from our sin to consider the path of new obedience. Hence, Calvin explained the evidence of repentance, saying that "the nature of the fruits of repentance" are "the duties of piety toward God, of charity toward men, and in the whole of life, holiness and purity." Thus, "the Spirit, while he urges us to repentance, often recalls us now to the individual precepts of the law."[15] Calvin leads us to see that repentance, as a work of the indwelling Spirit, not only causes us to sorrow over sin but also directs our attention to the duties of holiness that ought to characterize the faithful Christian life. That repentance is a matter of growing maturity throughout the Christian life is shown by how the catechism marks that we need "full *purpose* of, and *endeavor* after, new obedience." For this reason, Westminster Larger Catechism 76 addresses the topic of repentance just after its question about sanctification. Repentance is part of our ongoing life of sanctification wherein we pursue maturity in Christ. We must pursue this end of repentance, knowing that it is not fully realized at the beginning of the Christian life.

Repentance is necessary in the Christian life but not as a condition for Christ to accept us in the first place. We

---

14 Colquhoun, *Repentance*, 26-27.

15 Calvin, *Institutes*, 3.3.16.

come unto Christ for Him to make us better because we can never make ourselves better on our own. Hence, repentance is necessary because we have come to Christ, *not* as a way to come to Christ. In Westminster Confession 15.3, we find some help to express this relationship:

> Although repentance be not to be rested in, as any satisfaction for sin, or any cause of pardon thereof, which is the act of God's free grace in Christ; yet it is of such necessity to all sinners, that none may expect pardon without it.

Repentance does not make up for our sin, nor is it a reason that God forgives us. Still, it is so much of the Christian life's essence that we should not imagine that we are forgiven if we have no repentance in us.

Repentance must be part of our life for us to have confidence that we are forgiven. Despite what we might easily assume, that necessity does not mean the repentance comes before forgiveness of sin as a condition for it. This connection is like how petals relate to a flower. Petals do not give life to the flower. If a flower lacks petals, however, we have no reason to think that it has life. Roots give life to flowers, but petals must be there as fruit and evidence of life. Petals even come into existence after the roots because the roots are ultimately the reason that these petals exist. Still, these petals are necessary for us to expect that any life was in the flower.

Repentance bears the same relationship to forgiveness of sin. In a similar way that petals must be there as evidence to show that life is flowing from the roots into the flower, repentance must be present as evidence that we have received pardon for sin. Repentance does not *cause* the forgiveness of sin any more than petals cause roots. It is a sign of life that must be present in us if we are to have expectation that we have received pardon for our sin. Repentance does not even come before our sins are forgiven, since it is not a cause or condition. Rather, it sprouts from our new life as a blossom to adorn the forgiveness that we have received from Christ.

God grants this repentance as a gift of His grace. He grants it in the same way that He sovereignly bestows faith: by effectually calling us and giving the Spirit as a gift. As this gift of Spirit-wrought repentance directs our attention to the life we ought to live, it is repentance that guides our course toward taking full possession of the everlasting life granted to us by Christ. Christ has paved our course to everlasting life and has paved that path with repentance to show us the way.

The God-centered and Christ-focused character of repentance in Westminster Shorter Catechism 87 is also profoundly striking and worthy of greater reflection. Repentance grows "out of a true sense of his sin, *and apprehension of the mercy of God in Christ*," so that a sinner does "with grief and hatred of his sin, turn from it *unto God*, with full purpose of, and endeavor after, new obedience." Repentance is not simply turning from sin to new obedience. It is a turning *in view of God's mercy in Christ unto God*. In this turning to God because we have recognized and received His mercy given to us in Christ, we live in new obedience. Repentance is not merely turning from one set of behaviors to another—from sin to obedience. In repentance, we turn from one master to another—from sin to God in Christ, in view of the gospel mercy afforded us in Him (Matt. 6:24; Rom. 6:15-23). This apprehension of grace is the key to ensuring that repentance does not slide into a new, more religiously acceptable form of works righteousness. We are not simply turning to different works, but to God in Christ because of the gospel. Our obedience flows from our union and communion with Christ.[16]

Heidelberg Catechism 88–90 spells out in more detail what the second half of Westminster Shorter Catechism 87 says briefly. These questions resemble how Calvin nearly equated repentance with the whole of sanctification, in that they likewise highlight repentance as including the aspects of mortification and vivification.

> 88. What is the true repentance or conversion of man?
> It is the dying of the old nature and the coming to life of the new.
>
> 89. What is the dying of the old nature?
> It is to grieve with heartfelt sorrow that we have offended God by our sin, and more and more to hate it and flee from it.
>
> 90. What is the coming to life of the new nature?
> It is a heartfelt joy in God through Christ, and a love and delight to live according to the will of God in all good works.

Repentance is a change of our whole person, which of course results from the Spirit's work of grace in us. That change produces a hate for our sin and a desire to flee from it. Moreover, it also produces a joy and a delight in living in increasing holiness.

These confessional points encapsulate our emphasis on repentance as a blessing. Repentance is a gift of God's grace, given through the Spirit's indwelling presence. It is a welling up of the life bestowed upon us in Christ that makes us turn away from all that runs contrary to that life. God's gift of

16 Thanks to David Strain for this insight on Westminster Shorter 87 and whose language in personal correspondence, which I have borrowed, expressed the point so well.

repentance makes us recognize sin's putrid nature and how sin will lead only to our greater misery. Repentance leads only to a deeper experience of life given to us in Christ. It produces a heartfelt joy as God works in us, that we might live more and more in accord with how we were made to live as His image-bearers. Repentance is then the joyful, even if difficult, pursuit of greater delight in knowing greater freedom from sin's power. How does this traditional outlook on repentance help us embrace the joy of repentance?

Blessed Freedom

Our enjoyment comes, first, when we realize that God is providing freedom from sin's power as He grants us that gift of repentance. The pastoral concern on this front is to address that gravely mistaken assumption that repentance and sanctification is a demand of bleak necessity.

The right view of sin as a misery-causing enemy helps us to avoid pitfalls that lead to thinking of repentance as a joyless demand. Let's think about that staple practical joke toy – the spring-loaded snake in a can. When you pull the lid off, nothing can prevent that snake from leaping out! It is ready to be free. Repentance ought to be seen in this light—God is pulling the lid off and helping us leap from the confines of our sin. There should be nothing appealing about staying locked up in corruption. Let us be joyful to pounce forward in repentance, delightfully freed from our sin.

As a misery-inducing prison, sin has nothing good to offer us. Too often, I have heard pastors talk about people in their congregations as "wanting to have the best of both worlds." They mean that someone wants to have the great blessing of free salvation in Christ but also wants to enjoy all the fun things that sin offers. We need to realize that sin has no "best" to offer us. We have to challenge the very premise of the "best of both worlds" idea in recognizing that sin truly is miserable and offers no real satisfaction. If we believe that sin offers the "best" of some world, we will conclude that sanctification is the long, hard effort of giving up all the enjoyable things in life to become dour, dreary saints.

In reality, nothing could be farther from the truth. Repentance is in no way giving up anything good or even mediocre, much less anything best. Repentance is pursuing that which is wonderful and blessed. Jonathan Cruse spotlights this dynamic in observing, "Repentance is not about losing anything; it's about gaining the greatest thing imaginable: a deeper relationship with your Maker."[17] We know greater freedom in Christ and experience deeper delight in our walk with Him as we chase after true holiness and leave behind our misery-inducing sin. To thrive in the Christian life, we must believe that God wants *good* things for us. Even God's expectation that we must give up various things of our former life is for our good. Repentance, even when it is difficult, is the path of greatest joy.

We can easily be afraid of going to the dentist even when we know that we have a rotting tooth. Something makes us wary of sitting in that chair, fearing additional soreness and bad news, despite how we are painfully (literally) aware that we need help. Once that diseased tooth is removed though, life is full of blessed relief. Such is the case with sin. Repentance is God's gracious surgical work in our heart to remove infectious remnants of our old self. Though

17 Jonathan Landry Cruse, "You and Your King" (sermon delivered on January 28, 2024 at Community Presbyterian Church; accessed on February 15, 2024, https://www.sermonaudio.com/solo/kalamazoocpc/sermons/131242322575653/).

repentance can include some discomfort as we go through it, life becomes increasingly full of blessed relief as we are increasingly freed from our sin.[18]

We learn to foster this attitude as we recognize more fully that repentance is a gift of the gospel. As he instructed Timothy about the pastoral task of pursuing righteousness and the avoidance of divisions in church, Paul applied this principle in 2 Timothy 2:24-26:

> And the Lord's servant must not be quarrelsome but kind to everyone, able to teach, patiently enduring evil, correcting his opponents with gentleness. God may perhaps grant them repentance leading to a knowledge of the truth, and they may come to their senses and escape from the snare of the devil, after being captured by him to do his will.

Three quick points inform our consideration of repentance. First, pastors have a responsibility to correct error and sinful conduct *in a godly way*. Second, God often uses those efforts toward correction as a means to *grant* repentance. Third, repentance is God's gift to *escape* ways that the devil wants to harm us.

When we reflect upon these three points, we ought to see repentance more fully as God's gift for our good. The central premise is that God is the one who grants repentance. Just as He sovereignly calls us to faith in Christ, He sovereignly and graciously works repentance in us as a fruit of that faith. That gift of repentance, moreover, aims at our good. The devil has captured the unrepentant in a trap to do what he wants. Rest assured, the devil hates you and wants to make you miserable. Everything he offers you in sin is a trick to make you suffer.

---

18 Thanks to David Strain for suggesting this illustration.

When I was a kid, one of the main lessons I heard about navigating danger in the world was that I should never take candy from a stranger. The warning was about how sometimes bad people would use enticing things to lure you into terrible danger. What at first appears to be a kind and pleasing offer could quickly turn catastrophic. The stranger's offer of sweet reward only masks his intent to snare a child in order to inflict some sort of harm.

This warning illustrates exactly the way that the dynamics of temptation and repentance work out in our lives. The devil makes sin appear appealing as if it were a simple offer of tasty candy. Behind that offer is the intent to harm us in the deepest way. The sweet veneer of temptation is only a mask for dark purposes. While children may feel like we are squashing the fun by warning them not to take candy from strangers, it is truly for their good to keep them safe and free. When we realize the devil has only death in mind for us, we see how the admonition to repentance is ultimately about pursuing life and freedom out of the path of danger.

That reality of the devil's desires to snare us in his will stresses how God's gift of repentance aims at our freedom and our enjoyment of what is good. In repentance, God enables the repentant to "come to their senses" (2 Tim. 2:26). We might think of the prodigal son in Luke 15:11-32, as he was away from home reaping all the hard fallout of his sinful life. Then "when he came to himself" he realized how awful his sinful estate truly was, and he longed to be free of its misery and restored to his father (v. 17). The implication is that our lack of repentance, when we are convinced that sin is good and that indulgence of sin is the "best" of some world, is foolishness and false. The truth is that sin is horrible and ruinous. As God sanctifies and helps us to continue in repentance, He desires our enjoyment of all that is good as we learn to walk increasingly in the freedom of holiness. Repentance is not bleak but the pursuit of joyful freedom.

Fearless Freedom

Our enjoyment of repentance comes, second, when we realize that God is freeing us from sin's *power,* in light of how He has already freed us from sin's *penalty*. This book's second pastoral burden is to dispel fear from the process of repentance. In the twofold benefit of Christ, repentance as included in our sanctification is a blessing flowing *from*, not leading *to*, God's free declaration of pardon. In other words, God is presently freeing you from sin's power in sanctification because He has already freed you from its penalty in justification.

We need to process our need to pursue repentance rightly in light of God's mercy. We know that this obligation to repent and to grow in godliness belongs to the Christian life. We become fearful of the road of repentance, perhaps even paralyzed in it, when we buy the mistaken assumption that God's approval of us depends upon our repentance. The opposite is true, namely, that God's approval of us *drives* our repentance. He has bestowed new life on us in Christ, opened our eyes to see that sin is miserable, and given us the Spirit to spur—and help!—us on to increasing sanctification.

Where I live in Michigan, one great risk in driving at night is that deer might leap into your path. The likelihood of hitting a deer owes much to the deer's response to perceiving that it is in danger. When it sees the headlight of a car coming right at it, often it freezes, facing a paralysis of fear. Precisely because it freezes, the deer gets hit and may likely die.

Fear is the prime factor in that deer's demise. Of course, fear often paralyzes us too. If we are afraid of God as we live the Christian life, we are unlikely to make much progress in repentance. Rather, we will be frozen. We need a different framework than fear to keep us moving in repentance.

We must recognize that God joins His renewing work of sanctification to His legal act of justification. Sanctification is like the string hanging off the helium balloon of justification. God's declaration that we are righteous in His sight comes with His accompanying commitment to work true holiness in us. Calvin again helpfully explained the connection:

> Now if it is true – a fact abundantly clear – that that the whole of the gospel is contained under those two headings, repentance and forgiveness of sins, do we not see that the Lord freely justifies his own in order that he may at the same time restore them to true righteousness by sanctification of his Spirit?[19]

Calvin was most likely reflecting on passages such as Ephesians 1:4 and 2:8-10, which teach that the purpose and result of God's saving work is that we walk in good works. Thus, Calvin highlighted our point from above to dispel the mistake that the gospel offers free pardon but then demands obedience. Rather, the gospel offers forgiveness of sin and *also offers* new life of repentance and increasing obedience to God. That double offer is what it means to partake fully of life as it is offered holistically as the twofold benefit of Christ.

When we grasp that the summons to repentance as the path to greater freedom from sin's power is grounded in the reality that God has granted us total freedom from sin's penalty, we are enabled to pursue that repentant life with the

19 Calvin, *Institutes*, 3.3.19.

right perspective. Calvin drew upon the preaching of Jesus and John the Baptist to show that in their proclamation of the need to repent, they "derive the reason for repenting from grace itself and the promise of salvation."[20] The gospel offer again fuels our progress in repentance. The promise of salvation includes rescue from sin's power over our lives to enslave us in godlessness. When we see God's free, loving grace as the motivation for the pursuit of sanctification, we recognize that assurance of God's favor results in more faithfulness than any of our efforts that lack assurance or that are informed by lingering fear (1 John 4:18). As Calvin again related, "when we refer the origin of repentance to faith we do not imagine some space of time during which it brings it to birth; but we mean to show that a man cannot apply himself seriously to repentance without knowing himself to belong to God."[21] Further, "No one will gird himself willingly to observe the law but him who will be persuaded that God is pleased by his obedience."[22] When we know that the Judge who gives the law is our loving Father, we find ourselves delighted in pursuing the course of life that He sets before us for our good.

Conclusion

As the rest of this book explains, God's people are confronted with an ongoing need for repentance. One of the ways we reckon with this summons is that repentance, as it includes turning away from our sin, shows us that the Christian life has *more* to it than simply fire insurance to get us out of hell. It is certainly wonderful to have assurance of salvation, that we

20 Calvin, *Institutes*, 3.3.2.

21 Calvin, *Institutes*, 3.3.2.

22 Calvin, *Institutes*, 3.3.2.

will have everlasting life with God in the new creation waiting for us. But there is more to God's goodness than even that! He *frees* us from sin's tyranny *today* in this life. Sin is, after all, an affliction and we have emphasized that *misery* comes from sin.

As we explore the doctrine of repentance, one purpose is to see the resources on hand to help us repent. Perhaps our *first* reaction to someone struggling with temptation and sin should not be to call their salvation into question. Perhaps, it should be enough to start by asking, "Do you like being miserable?" We have the answer: "If you don't like it, then repent. It's better to enjoy the Lord more."

The following five expositional reflections on repentance then in some way circle around the idea that sanctification is good in itself. It is freedom. People who cherish Christ long to be like Him. Obviously, it is intrinsically good to be like Christ. We do not need to tie some higher result on top of sanctification than being progressively made into the image of God's Son. Nothing can trump that blessedness. What a wonderful thing to resemble the character of God's Son with ever increasing fullness!

Those called by Christ's name and baptized into His body should hunger and thirst for righteousness for all these reasons and more. We have that desire not foremost because we are scared of what might happen if we do not get it together. Foremost, we understand that there is goodness in righteousness and there is freedom in repentance. We should not need a payoff for our sanctification other than the blessing it is on its own.

Chapter Two

THE REPENTANT LIFE

2 Corinthians 7:8-11

When I was a small boy, I took a trip out to my uncle's lake house. In the pivotal moment on this trip, I was standing on a big platform on the dock hanging over the water—this giant raised platform was made for jumping into the water. When I was small, the distance to the water made me feel like I must have been higher than an astronaut in space. My family later told me that they never thought I would jump because it seemed so high. For sure, I had to fortify myself to have the nerve to leap from the perch of safety. Despite my terror, I did it. Sure enough, once I jumped the first time, I found out how much I enjoyed it and went back repeatedly.

As we think together about repentance, let us hope to find a similar experience in overcoming initial fears to find great satisfaction. Truly facing and admitting our sin can be one of the scariest things in the world. Still, just because it may initially scare us does not mean it should not be done.

A reminder about the God-centered, Christ-focused character of repentance from Westminster Shorter Catechism 87 helps us keep the right bearings. Repentance includes a turning from our sin unto God with full purpose after new obedience because of our "apprehension of the mercy of God in Christ." That awareness that God has been merciful to us through the gospel as He receives us in Christ fuels our efforts at repentance. The reality of our belonging *to* Christ is then foundational and formative for how we live *for* Christ as the response to His grace.

That insight shows how the gospel motivates us to turn to God to be free from sin. In repentance, we are not turning from sin into empty air. We turn *to God*. We turn to the God who has been merciful to us in Christ. In that opening anecdote about jumping into the lake, if we substituted the lake of dark, murky water with a lake of a milkshake, the situation seems far less threatening. I ought even to have been enticed to leap from that platform into the lake of sweetness. Repentance ought to seem like this version of the story in that we ought to see the sweetness of Christ before us as we turn to God on account of the gospel, leaving sin behind. The gospel realities of belonging to Christ ought to form our response to our sin.

Hence, we need to look to God's Word to tell us how we should react to our sin. In 2 Corinthians 7:8-11, Paul outlined two kinds of grief. He acknowledged that one sort of grief is when we feel bad for being criticized or when we suffer unpleasant consequences for our actions. In this form, we grieve because we dislike what happens to us. By contrast, the other sort of grief is a godly grief containing an earnestness to put away sin and to be zealous for a renewed life. Whereas worldly grief hates what happens to me because of my actions, godly grief hates what I have done inasmuch as my sin has offended the true and holy God.

Scripture is clear that we must hate our sin. The way forward in hating our sin often means admitting to ourselves and owning up to others about how heinously we have conducted ourselves. One hymn gives voice to this sense before the Lord:

> Before thee, God, who knowest all,
> with grief and shame I prostrate fall.
> I see my sins against thee, Lord,
> the sins of thought, of deed, and word.
> They press me sore; I cry to thee:
> O God, be merciful to me![1]

Repentance very much means that we have to say goodbye to saving face—at least in a worldly sense. That step can feel very much like standing on that platform above the lake, afraid to launch yourself into the air for an uncontrolled freefall. Still, if we understand that repentance is a saving *grace* from God, we will recognize that much good comes out of overcoming our fear. The right understanding of repentance helps us to be people who hate our sin. When this hatred develops, we quit caring about saving *our* face and start caring about seeking *God's* face by destroying the sin of our hearts as thoroughly as we can this side of heaven.

How might repentance come to bear upon our lives? What features of repentance guide us to see that it is worth overcoming our fears to step into this posture and practice? We can remind ourselves how Westminster Shorter Catechism 87 explains it: "Repentance unto life is a saving grace, whereby a sinner, out of a true sense of his sin, and apprehension of the mercy of God in Christ, does, with grief

1 Magnus B. Landstad, "Before Thee, God, Who Knowest All," *Trinity Psalter Hymnal*, 177.

and hatred of his sin, turn from it unto God, with full purpose of, and endeavor after, new obedience." Repentance includes two things: putting sin to death and bringing godliness to life. It means turning away from what is wrong and turning toward what is right. Inasmuch as sin makes us miserable, we ought to know how good it will be to overcome our fears because repentance is a major step away from misery.

We can be less fearful of repentance also because we do not have to get it exactly right the first time. Since repentance involves admitting our faults, we can be ready to admit the fault even in our repentance. As said in a classic puritan prayer, "I need to repent of my repentance."[2] We get better as we practice it over time.

We imbibe that truth more easily when we see that repentance is a posture as well as a practice. In the first of his famous Ninety-Five Theses that famously started the Protestant Reformation, Martin Luther wrote, "When our Lord and Master Jesus Christ said, 'Repent,' he willed the entire life of believers to be one of repentance."[3] Luther highlighted the *ongoing* need for repentance, helping us to see that we never grow beyond repenting nor diminish it down to a mere act.

All these considerations show us that repentance is a permanent, essential, and prominent aspect of what it means to live the Christian life. Hence this chapter is about how we need a deeper sense of real, thorough, and obvious repentance. It sets out to describe more fully what repentance is and how to take steps toward it.

---

2 "Continual Repentance," in Arthur Bennett (ed.), *The Valley of Vision: A Collection of Puritan Prayers and Devotions* (The Banner of Truth Trust, 1975), 136.

3 Martin Luther, "The Ninety-Five Theses," in Timothy F. Lull (ed.), *Martin Luther's Basic Theological Writings*, 2nd ed. (Fortress Press, 2005), 41.

Describing Repentance

How can we expand our understanding of repentance? As we already hinted, people sometimes assume that repentance means feeling bad. In some ways, feeling bad may be part of repentance but it is certainly not a thorough understanding. To get a right sense of repentance, we return to those two kinds of grief in 2 Corinthians 7:8-11.

Grief that Matters

The Corinthians needed to see that they could not dilute repentance into merely unpleasant feelings. In verses 8-9, Paul wrote, "For even if I made you grieve with my letter, I do not regret it—though I did regret it, for I see that that letter grieved you, though only for a while. As it is, I rejoice, not because you were grieved, but because you were grieved into repenting. For you felt a godly grief, so that you suffered no loss through us." Several considerations grow out of this section.

First, Paul had previously written to the church in Corinth, and that earlier letter grieved them. In other words, that letter had some sting to it, which the Corinthians had felt. In one way, he was sorry that they had been grieved but, in another sense, he was glad because it produced repentance.

We can apply that observation quickly on its own. We should see that we cannot always avoid uncomfortable things if we are going to be faithful in the Christian life or in any ministry the Lord may give us. Paul himself found it difficult when he had to say hard things to other believers for whom he cared deeply. He also knew that he had to follow through and say those hard things. If he did not, they would not flourish spiritually. We see then that not everything that is ultimately good is experientially comfortable. Concerning repentance, we recognize that discomfort will occur as we realize our sin, as we are rebuffed for our sin, and as we rebuke others for their sin. We should be uncomfortable. We should also do what is right.

Second, mark how Paul saw a difference between grieving—feeling bad—and repenting. Feeling bad does not exhaust repentance. Repentance will certainly include some sort of emotional component. That component is not *all* that repentance is though. Paul said that the Corinthians were grieved into repenting, meaning that repentance is something deeper than feeling bad.

We can see what else repentance involves as we move ahead in the passage. Repentance does contain *a godly grief*. As we learn in 2 Corinthians 7:10, even that godly grief is not simply feeling bad: "For godly grief produces a repentance that leads to salvation without regret, whereas worldly grief produces death." Godly grief is distinct from worldly grief.

How many times did we face this situation as children when our parents confronted us with our wrongdoing? We are familiar with the forced apology: "Say you're sorry." After offering that apology, the frequent follow-up twisted the screws even tighter: "Are you truly sorry, or are you just sorry that you got in trouble?" The answer was usually obvious.

That problem of regretting the consequence but not the sin fills our world. People do not lament their promiscuity but only that they contracted diseases or selfishly regret that they now have responsibility for a child. People are not sorry that they stole from others and even ruined lives by swindling retirement funds and investments, but they are sorry that they got jail time for it. So often we grieve what happens to us because of our sin but do not grieve that we committed our sin.

True repentance means that we learn to hate it when our thoughts, words, and deeds are displeasing to God and go against what is good. People may feel bad about what they did because they regret the consequences. That sort of grief does not mean that they despise the heinousness of their actions that wrong God and other people. That sort of grief is the worldly kind. We must strive for the godly grief that laments over how we have used our mental, emotional, and physical abilities to wrong God and wrong other people made in God's image.

God-Given Sorrow

When God works repentance in His people, it is not superficial but deep and extends to causing them to hate their own sinfulness. Ezekiel 36:26-27 describes God's renewing work: "And I will give you a new heart, and a new spirit I will put within you. And I will remove the heart of stone from your flesh and give you a heart of flesh. And I will put my Spirit within you, and cause you to walk in my statutes and be careful to obey my rules." As Ezekiel continued, he named specific effects of that renewal, stating in verse 31: "Then you will remember your evil ways, and your deeds that were not good, and you will *loathe yourselves* for your iniquities and your abominations." God's work of repentance includes this realization that what I have done is truly detestable, even regardless of what consequences I may or may not experience because of it.

When I was young, I never understood why my mom was always so concerned about stains on my clothes. In recent years, I find myself deeply frustrated if I find a spot on one of my favorite shirts that seems guaranteed not to come out. I have grown more aware of what is embarrassing.

The embarrassment is clearer to me because I understand better that a stain disfigures a shirt.

Before the Lord works in us, we do not have spiritual understanding that our sin disfigures us before Him. When He works repentance in us, we come to see the problem with all the stains on our life. We realize that they are not only embarrassing but even shameful. The Lord opens our eyes to understand why we should hate our sin.

God will not work in His own people simply a regret for doing bad things, but He will also work a genuine hatred for sin and a love for righteousness. In our day that is obsessed with self-esteem and avoiding shame, Ezekiel's point that repentance will look like loathing ourselves for our transgressions needs more explanation. People might easily let it resonate in wrong directions. They might also take issue with it for exactly what it means. Ezekiel was not shaming people for the cultural reasons so popular today, as if they were not physically attractive enough or their skills were inadequate. He was not sending them to hate themselves for their personalities or the like. He said they will hate themselves over *their sin*. Their wrongdoings would overwhelm them. They would realize how heinously they have lived and come to detest it.

In that regard, we rejoice that God works repentance. His promise through Ezekiel of a new heart enables us to turn from sin and live otherwise, albeit imperfectly. Although realization of our sin causes us to hate it, God works in us so that we do more than hate sin: we flee from it. Repentance is a saving grace where we are enabled to turn away from all we hate about who we have been and what we have done so that we can be and do something better. In repentance, God gives us a deep and real hatred of sin as well as a true and earnest hunger for holiness.

Difficulties in Repentance

With that description in place, what might prevent our repentance? What might keep us out of the penitent posture or from embracing the practice of repentance? Those questions could have a thousand answers. Each of us differs in our temptations and weaknesses. So, we will be helped by focusing on two principles that foster our avoidance of repentance: we tend to externalize and excuse our own sin.

Externalizing Sin

Christians often highlight how sinful our surrounding culture is. Certainly, good reasons abound for lamenting the state of western society and its drift away from shared assumptions taken from Christianity. Nonetheless, cultures are not abstract forces that become sinful apart from the people living in it who adopt sinful values and commit sinful practices. Cultures are comprised of people, and a culture is sinful when its people are sinful. Because sinfulness is tied concretely to people rather than abstractly to a culture, cultures cannot repent in any meaningful sense other than widespread repentance among its citizens.

Moaning about culture is one way that we externalize sin. By identifying a difficulty that hinders our posture and practice of repentance, we are simply marking sin *out there,* while not perceiving our own rebelliousness against the Lord. Too often, we can use our laments about the culture's sinfulness to distract from or even neglect lamenting how sinful we are personally. Obviously, cultures are in rebellion against God in the sense highlighted above, but we will profit far more from searching out and eradicating our sin than from droning about how bad they are out there.

This externalizing of sin is a symptom of an underlying root that wants to project the problem onto others without taking responsibility for our own wrongdoings. We presume that it's "they," the others, who are truly sinful, not us. We place ourselves in the position of being beyond reproach and cast aspersions on others. It rehashes Adam's "the-woman-you-gave-me" tactic when he tried to blame Eve—and arguably even God Himself—for his sin (Gen. 3:12).

The cultural perspective was an easy entryway into this problem, but it works out in other day-to-day ways as well. How often do we do the same thing in our relationships, especially when we get into an argument? We can so plainly see how the other person is wrong and are so ready to point out what we see as their sin. All the while, we overlook our own sinfulness in the matter. Even with our closest family and friends, we leap to externalize sin by seeing how wrong they are while neglecting to search ourselves deeply.

We should place a priority on personal repentance. Without a doubt, we ought to address outside issues—be that cultural or another individual—in ways and at times that are appropriate and helpful. All the same, we gain far more ground by being a repentant people than by calling others to repent.

Holy Scripture calls us to consider our own hearts as ground zero for sinfulness and to give careful consideration to our own repentance even in relation to others. In Matthew 7:1-15, Jesus taught:

> Judge not, that you be not judged. For with the judgment you pronounce you will be judged, and with the measure

> you use it will be measured to you. Why do you see the speck that is in your brother's eye, but do not notice the log that is in your own eye? Or how can you say to your brother, 'Let me take the speck out of your eye,' when there is the log in your own eye? You hypocrite, first take the log out of your own eye, and then you will see clearly to take the speck out of your brother's eye.

Christ Himself was pinpointing the problem of externalizing sin, as the hypocrite in question could so easily perceive the sin outside himself while missing how his own was much worse. Although many have abused Christ's injunction to "judge not," we cannot circumvent its right use. Let us be quick to see our own sin and be vigilantly ready to recognize how we must repent.

The point comes home even regarding the church's relationship to the wider culture. After all, Scripture tells us in 1 Peter 4:17 that judgment will start with God's own house: "For it is time for judgment to begin at the household of God; and if it begins with us, what will be the outcome for those who do not obey the gospel of God?" Peter's point is not that we should be ignorant of a culture's ecosystem of sin as if we are to ignore the problems of godlessness that can surround us. Even though we should not be naïve nor negligent on this front, we should tend most to our own affairs, dealing with our significant personal wickedness. I should quit worrying so much about how bad *they* are and start worrying about how bad *I* am. It is fitting that every Christian give first attention to whether he or she is living his or her own life in a fashion that is generally pleasing before the Lord.

Excusing Sin

Another difficulty is that we often fail to reckon with how far short we personally can truly fall in the Christian life. For sure, this issue is related to externalizing sin in that whether excusing or externalizing comes first in our hearts, one often enables the other. Many of us can slip into the presumptuous pattern of thinking that we are basically alright. The danger therein is that we diminish our own wrongdoings and eventually fail to see them at all. We excuse our own transgressions and cease to repent over them.

Christians readily admit that they are *generally* sinful and imperfect but often flinch at talking about being a sinner *specifically* in certain ways. I like to keep my sinfulness at arm's length away from what I have actually done. One way in vogue to distance ourselves from our sin is by talking about "brokenness." Truly, brokenness has a place in explaining our experience in a sinful world. If we mean that we are broken as in "contrite" because we see that we are sinners, that is a wonderful place to have reached spiritually. Often, however, "brokenness" refers to the generic problems of the world. We might talk about how we are broken and struggling, which is also meant to imply that it is alright to accept and indulge our moral faults. My faults are just a bug in my system caused by my brokenness rather than volitional rebellion against God and His law.

The truth is that we are more than broken. We are treasonous rebels. Sin does not just happen to us. We commit sin. Brokenness truly exists, and many cases do require pastoral sensitivity to those factors. We must all also see that we need to own our sin and cannot excuse it as some acceptable glitch of an imperfect world.

We should work at identifying the ways that we dodge recognizing and owning our own sin, so that we can instead target and attack it. In my family growing up, one standard feature of an argument was for someone to say, "Well, I guess that I'm just a terrible person." This exclamation was supposed to be the trump card to make the other person say, "NO! It's fine now, don't feel bad. You're wonderful." I'm that frustrating fly in the family ointment because I tend to say, "Well, yes I know that, but so am I, and we still have to resolve this problem." We need to reckon more with the way that we are sinful people. We should admit it more starkly.

The difficulties in repentance are in how we try to avoid how sinful we are. We must be more conscious of Jesus' "golden rule" about how we should treat others in the same way that we want to be treated (Luke 6:31). We usually want others to treat us graciously and with a tender touch about our sins and faults. Thus, we learn that repentance means that, even as we perceive and must address others in their sin, we must do so in the spirit of gentleness with the goal of restoration (Gal. 6:1-2). We should not deceive ourselves that our sin is a trivial matter, while thinking that everyone else's is nuclear level in need of *my* rebuke (Gal. 6:3-5). We should search ourselves for reasons to repent and only then, in light of how we would want others to help us in our repentance, confront others in their sins and shortcomings. Finding our own need for grace helps us to give grace to others.

Doing Repentance

What does the posture and practice of repentance look like in regular application? Our preceding consideration of what repentance is and difficulties that hinder it are all well and good, but how do I work this truth out in my life?

More than anything else, we must make a conscious commitment to be repentant. We should ready ourselves to repent to someone else. We do not have the right to write off repentance as an outdated practice or as something fit for only the Grade A sins. We must accept that Scripture enjoins us to *act* in repentance. The implications of that foundation have many layers.

Repenting to God

Fundamentally, we direct our repentance toward God by praying more often in focused confession of sin. Although we should avoid endless and morbid introspection, we should search ourselves to repent before the Lord. Westminster Confession of Faith 15.5 explains: "Men ought not to content themselves with a general repentance, but it is every man's duty to endeavor to repent *of his particular sins, particularly*." We ought to be ready to name our specific transgressions and ask God to cover them in Christ's blood so that we have His forgiveness (Ps. 19:13; Luke 19:8; 1 Tim. 1:12-15).

Repenting to One Another

We should also be ready to repent to other people. Protestants cherish our doctrine of Christ's priesthood wherein we affirm that Jesus is our *only* Mediator and that we can go directly to God on account of Christ's work to confess our sin. We still are called, however, to repent to our brothers and sisters when it is needed, helpful, or appropriate. James 5:16 explicitly teaches us to "confess your sins *to one another* and pray for one another, that you may be healed." Westminster Confession 15.6 applies this teaching, holding it together with what we saw just above: "As every man is bound to make private confession of his sins to God, praying for the pardon thereof…so, he that scandalizes his brother, or the church of Christ, ought to be willing, by private or public confession, and sorrow for his sin, to declare his repentance to those that are offended." As the Confession then notes, that repentance to one another ought to result in our mutual reconciliation. In sum, our beautiful privilege of confessing our sins directly to God should not be a bulwark or excuse against repenting to or before one another when it is fitting.

James' teaching to confess our sins to someone else is very uncomfortable. The right application is not that you should run around spraying everyone you know fire-hose style with admission of all your transgression. Still, God has plainly instructed confession as part of the Christian life. We need a sense of why it might be good for us because James said to do it for *healing*. It is restorative.

How so? God is of course the one who forgives sin, and we can go directly to God in prayer. In this life, however, we cannot *see* God. Many times, we are helped and comforted by witnessing the concrete response of a brother or sister extending grace to us. Consider again the exhortation in Galatians 6:1-2: "Brothers, if anyone is caught in any transgression, you who are spiritual should restore him in a spirit of gentleness. Keep watch on yourself, lest you too be tempted. Bear one another's burdens, and so fulfill the law of Christ." Carrying one another's burdens, as we mutually fight against sin, includes this help: that we will manifestly experience grace from one another as we openly repent and find acceptance. Repenting to someone else, therefore, is not a punishment for sin. It is a help to give support, encouragement, and accountability. If someone is treating your repentance otherwise, that itself is a problem that should be addressed because we should find healing and help in confessing to one another.

We can now consider two more pointed takeaways about what repentance can look like.

Don't Explain Away Sin

Our culture thinks there is a reason behind all that we do, meaning most people think that having an explanation for our actions makes them alright. Christians should not be that way. We should be people characterized by humility. Make no mistake: the repentant life requires immense humility.

For that reason, our first application is not to explain away our wrongdoings. When someone tells you that you have wronged them, you should respond, "I'm sorry." Our apologies for sins and offenses committed should end with a full stop. They should ordinarily have no qualification, no self-protection, no explanation, but just an apology. When someone points out that you need to adjust a specific feature of your life, seriously consider it and talk through it. We drift towards blaming other people and external factors for our failures. Christians should *at least consider* that if someone suggests a failure, they might be right. So, we should quit trying to make it better and just admit our wrongs.

We might be afraid that our quickness to repent might be used against us. Certainly, wisdom is needed in different contexts to measure what it means to take responsibility for your actions in responsible ways. Unless you work at a Christian organization, being so forthcoming with the spiritual components of some shortcoming in your job might not be very fitting. Still, even if we might fear repercussions, we know that the right thing to do is to be honest about ways that we truly failed in our job performance rather than dishonestly defending ourselves, making endless excuses, or blaming someone else. Of course, context should affect how we put this posture of repentance into practice in specific ways.

More pointedly, we might fear that, if we are repentant among our fellow saints at church, we will not receive the grace from them that they should extend as fellow sinners in need of mercy. The hard aspect is that the fear that other people might not do what is right should not prevent us from doing what is right. We cannot justly avoid due repentance over our sin just because someone else might not understand how Christians are supposed to reciprocate grace to one another. The right thing to do remains the right thing to do.

The church functioning well as the church is an influential factor in this issue. The church ought to be in favor of reconciliation and restoration wherever it is possible. If a church favors ostracization of those who admit their sin rather than helping them to overcome it, it is not a healthy church. You do not want to be there anyway. The church ought to be fostering a culture of forgiveness and mutual acceptance as we labor forward together.

Lead with Repentance

Whereas the first application was more concerned with our response when we are confronted by someone else, sometimes we are the ones who have the grievance against others. How do we maintain robust repentance when we have the supposed upper hand? A dear friend of mine, Matt Francisco, who has mentored and helped me since college, often told me, "Lead with repentance." In many cases, when I have something against someone else, I should put confronting them on pause until I am ready to open by stating my sin. Rarely am I without guilt, even if that is merely over some growing bitterness about how I was wronged.

God's grace towards us helps us to show grace to those who have wronged us. In Ephesians 4:32, Paul drew on this point to explain how we ought to go about forgiving one another: "Be kind to one another, tenderhearted, forgiving one another, *as God in Christ forgave you*." Christians must forgive one another emphatically "as God in Christ forgave you," meaning *in the same way* that God grants us forgiveness. Christian, let us never forget that God forgives you by looking at Christ's sacrifice on the cross as satisfying any justice owed for the wrongdoing. We are called to forgive on that basis too. We forgive others by looking at Christ's cross where any wrong done to us by other Christians has been punished and forgiven. We should remember too that all our sins were also reasons that Christ died. This aspect of repentance is just another way of reminding ourselves that we repent because we have apprehended God's mercy to us in Christ. The grace of the gospel fuels our repentance before God and how we can forgive others.

Drawing this biblical material together helps us see why we should lead with repentance even when we are the one confronting someone else about their need to repent. We ought to be quick to reconcile and quick to forgive. We should long for renewed relationship. Therefore, I ordinarily ought to confess my sin first. In most situations, both people have sinned. So, be ready to confess your side of the wrongdoing.

This approach also has a practical aspect. Take, for example, this way of opening a hard conversation: "I must confess that I have grown bitter with you. I know that I need your forgiveness for that. And I need to tell you that I was really hurt when you…" If that person responds with "Yeah, well, you were wrong to…," you have already addressed that problem. You can say, "Yes, I have repented. I know I am sinful. I hope we might consider how we can *both* turn away from our shortcomings though." Leading with repentance helps to short-circuit accusation. Counter arguments struggle to get off the ground when they are running against the current of humility and repentance.

Still, let us be mindful of a warning to watch our motives as we lead with repentance, knowing that it might have this practical benefit. Potentially, we could lead with confessing our own sin while thinking the *real* problem is only with the other person. We might even be using our sin simply as a launching point to get to the real reason that we are talking to the other person, namely, to confront them. In this case, our motive is not sincere.[4] We must be careful to watch our hearts to be diligent in wanting to repent of our sin to deal truly with our own wrongdoings, not just to have an excuse to rebuke someone else.

Conclusion

Even though repentance can be very uncomfortable for us, much beauty resides in it. Repentance is sweet because it is grounded in the gospel; hence Westminster Confession 15.1 calls it, "an evangelical grace." The gospel—the evangel—provides grace that has a tremendous affect upon our lives. John Colquhoun explains how *evangelical* repentance differs from *legal* repentance (the regret for sin's consequences) because "It is a gracious principle and habit implanted in the soul by the Spirit of Christ, in the exercise of which a regenerate and believing sinner, deeply sensible of the

4 Thanks to Craig Troxel for this caveat.

exceeding sinfulness and just demerit of his innumerable sins, is truly humbled and grieved before the Lord, on account of the sinfulness and hurtfulness of them."[5] Further, the exercise of repentance "is either under the law as a covenant of works, and the domination of a legal spirit; or under the influence of the covenant of grace, and of an evangelical spirit."[6] Believers have the Spirit working repentance in them because the Spirit's indwelling is a gift of the gospel (Eph. 1:13-14). As God further uses the proclaimed gospel to shape our lives, the Spirit works to make its grace-giving effects further our freedom from sin's grip upon us.[7] Repentance is an evangelical grace because the gospel enables us to turn away from our sin to seek Christ increasingly. Certainly, to seek Christ is a sweet reality.

This aspect of repentance as an evangelical grace reminds us why it is good to embrace our need to confess and fight our sin. Every time that we want to avoid feeling the weight of how bad our transgressions are, we should remember that Jesus died only for terrible people. Jesus did not die for those who are well, but for those who are dead, to bring them to life. Repentance sets us free because it casts us back into the arms of Christ who receives and renews contrite sinners. In *this way*, as Paul noted in 2 Corinthians 7:10, repentance leads to salvation by pushing us continually to Christ's mercy. God opposes the proud, but Jesus has died for those who come to Him for forgiveness. So, let us throw ourselves in faith on this Savior who bought sinners and gives them everlasting life.

---

5 Colquhoun, *Repentance*, 2.

6 Colquhoun, *Repentance*, 150.

7 Colquhoun, *Repentance*, 7-8.

Chapter Three

A PATTERN OF PENITENCE

Psalm 38

I have no clue how to buy fruit. The principles for assessing fruit's ripeness and readiness for purchase are basically lost on me. Thousands of rules seem to apply about whether this fruit is supposed to be soft when you push it or that fruit is supposed to be firm when squeezed. I struggle to know whether the piece of fruit that I'm holding even counts as soft or firm, and even more to know whether it ought to be squishy or rigid to be fit for purchase. Each piece of fruit requires its own special assessment about what to do when it proves to be soft or firm.

Fruit has its wide variations for soft and firm, and people have a similar spectrum of hardness about processing their need to repent. Some people have tender consciences, lamenting deeply over the smallest sin. Others have hard hearts—stubborn consciences—being often unable to see their wrong even while committing serious sin. Further, we easily overlook confused consciences that tend to know their sin and when they commit it but seem to think that no one else can see it. They seem to assume that the best solution is to hide their sin, excuse it, or blame others for it, rather than admit, own, and deal with it. Like every piece of fruit requires its own assessment about how soft or firm it is, every conscience likewise demands that specific attention.

Psalm 38 helps us think through that issue of varying consciences. One purpose for which God inspired the Psalter is for our instruction about the godly response to the entire spectrum of experience and emotion that we encounter in the Christian life. The Book of Psalms contains different genres including psalms of praise, thanksgiving, and lament. Psalm 38 is a psalm of repentance and should, therefore, help us think about what it means to have an open, repentant conscience, as well as how to process our need to repent in light of however hard or tender our consciences might presently be.

This psalm models repentance in that David knew the reality of his sin, its consequences, and how it should shape his relationships. As with most psalms, we don't know the precise background for when David wrote this one. Perhaps that ignorance is helpful in this instance, however, because we can consider its details as a pattern to shape the godly response to the realization of our sin in any situation. This chapter then explores how we must tune our consciences to search and understand our own sin so that we can repent well.

Repentance Prompted by Discipline

In Psalm 38, David modeled clarity in thinking about our own sin, its consequences, and what we should do. His pattern teaches us how our experience of the Lord's discipline on account of our sin ought to bring us to repentance.

Structurally, Psalm 38 is two laments bookended by two pleas for mercy. David's opening petition in verses 1-2 was for God's hard discipline to ease. In verses 3-10, David lamented how his sin brought illness upon himself. Then, in verses 11-20, he lamented how his sin had created problems in his relationships. He closed in verses 21-22 by seeking the Lord not to forsake him and to provide quick deliverance—the second plea for mercy. What's the point of this structure? We see that the biggest section of the psalm is about David's grief over how much his sin had ruined things, not in prayers for God's mercy! David exemplifies the point made in Westminster Shorter Catechism 87 that "a true sense of his sin" helped him to have "apprehension of the mercy of God in Christ." We see God's mercy as sweeter when we have truly recognized it as relief for our need.

Basics of Identifying Sin

David's self-awareness of his sin in Psalm 38 provides a lens for what balanced repentance should be like. He opened in verses 1-2 by expressing repentance: "O Lord, rebuke me not in your anger, nor discipline me in your wrath! For your arrows have sunk into me, and your hand has come down on me." David knew that his sin deserved God's punishment, since, as later verses show, God had already distributed corrective discipline.

As he acknowledged that the Lord's hard discipline had registered with him, he prayed that God would no longer inflict what is due. As his prayer continued, he admitted that he was in no position to reject God's discipline—but, understandably, he wished not to receive it any further. God had made His point, and David knew that God's heavy-handedness was meant to chastise Him.

We need to learn to take account of our lives and to measure them in light of the Lord's providence. In Psalm 38, David's self-awareness about his sin included understanding that his sin had caused his present suffering. So, here we find a principle that repentance includes conscientiousness that we have done wrong and that our wrongdoing deserves God's wrathful response. Sometimes we dislike admitting this connection. We wish instead to shoulder it away by saying that, since we are all imperfect, not every sin warrants that God's hand would crush us. David, however, under the Spirit's inspiration, readily admitted that God had laid His disciplinary hand upon him so hard that it felt like arrows had pierced him. David knew that these arrows came from God Himself and that they were the consequences for his sin. Later, we will round out this application to obtain that desired balance, but the point stands that we should be willing to recognize that our sin is sometimes the cause of our hardship.

The necessary point to grasp is how David had a realistic sense of the extent of his sin and the consequences it brought. The first section details the suffering he feels because he knew that, whatever the illness that had come upon him, it was connected to his sin. Verse 3 marked the Lord's discipline upon his sin: "There is no soundness in my flesh *because of your indignation*; there is no health in my bones *because of my sin*" (emphasis added). One commentator translated verse 5: "My wounds stink and fester *because of my stupidity*," which certainly helps draw attention to David's raw disgust of himself and his honesty about how personally degraded he was.[1] We may not know what illness beset David as he

1 John Goldingay, *Psalms*, 3 vols. (Baker Commentary on the Old Testament Wisdom and Psalms; Baker Academic, 2006–8), 1:542 (emphasis added).

wrote and, for our purposes, we do not need to work in detail through each expression of his symptoms. We simply need to see that David understood that, in this particular instance, he was sick because of sin.

Balancing the Issue of Disciplinary Hardship

We should add some balance points. The Book of Job shows that we should not assume that every calamity that happens to us is a direct consequence of our own sin. Jesus was explicit that the blind man whom He healed in John 9 was not afflicted because of his own sin.[2] That caveat is necessary because we must maintain a measured and tempered approach to assessing our hardship in relation to our sin concerning whether it is the Lord's discipline for our sin. A few clarifications are in order.

First, David *knew* that his sin had caused his illness. He wrote Psalm 38 with a Spirit-induced, conscious awareness that his sin had brought about this consequence. Sometimes in our lives, we can make such a clear connection. If I were to consume too much alcohol and drive, then receive a legal penalty for it, the direct cause-and-effect relationship for that consequence is clear. Even for illnesses, if someone commits adultery and in doing so contracts a sexually transmitted disease, the direct cause and effect relation of sin to hardship is plainly obvious. It is then *possible* that our sin has directly caused our hardship.

Second, speculation about whether our sin has caused our hardship when the direct cause-effect relationship is not obvious is unwise. If the connection of our sin to our hardship as God's disciplinary action is plain, then we should

2 Thanks to Scott Clark, Jonathan Cruse, and David Strain for suggesting the relevance of John 9 on this point.

own it as such. The Scripture provides examples of this sort of situation not only in Psalm 38 but also in Psalm 3 where, as the heading states, David's persecution was the result of his sins of adultery with Bathsheba and murder of Uriah. In both cases, the Lord Himself made clear to David that his specific sin was the reason for those specific afflictions.

On the other hand, Psalm 6 contains similar laments to Psalm 38 about illness and physical affliction but lacks any statement of self-awareness that sin has caused the same sort of hardship. Psalm 6 then instructs us how to pray seeking God's help for this sort of affliction when we cannot see any connection between our trial and our sin. As noted already, Job's protracted and very painful hardship was not in any way the repercussion for specific sins that he had committed. These biblical precedents show that we must seek the Lord and bring our hardship to Him without speculating about why he would bring this difficulty upon us unless it is plainly clear. If our hardship seems to come out of the blue, without an obvious connection to a specific sin from the human perspective, we avoid spiraling into endless introspection about what sin has brought our present affliction upon us.

The upshot of holding Psalm 38 and Psalm 6 together is that we ought to seek the Lord's help in all circumstances and run to Him in our plight. We are meant to seek the Lord whether we have brought our trouble upon ourselves or have no idea why we face the difficulties that have entered our lives. Whether we pray seeing a connection to our sin or without any awareness of how or if our sin relates, our affliction always occurs in God's providence as He cares for and even disciplines us. In relation to repentance, this balance helps us see that we should be open to the possibility that our sin has brought on our trial, but we should not always presume that our hardship is the Lord's disciplinary action against us when the connection to our sin is not plain.

The ambiguous background to Psalm 38 leaves us with those principles of considering ourselves, our sin, and our hardship without committing us to the certainty of one conclusion. Despite lots of scholarship on the psalms, we do not know what sickness plagued David. We also cannot discern what his sin was in this instance. In verse 4, we can see that David knew he was entrenched in his sin, and God brought him to a halt by afflicting him: "For my iniquities have gone over my head; like a heavy burden, they are too heavy for me." The metaphor alludes to water as if David was immersed in his sin, which had overwhelmed him. So, we know that his sin was serious, and that he was not just guessing why he was ill. He knew that he was trapped in this specific sin and that the Lord was disciplining him to break him free from his chains of temptation.

Bigger Perspectives

Illness is not the only way that the Lord's discipline can work to break us free from our seasons of entrenched sin. In Psalm 38:11-20, David described how his sin had turned his friends against him and created a host of enemies. In verses 17-18, he repented in light of how his foes were mounting their plans against him, "For I am ready to fall, and my pain is ever before me. *I confess my iniquity; I am sorry for my sin.*" He again saw that his trouble was because of his own sin.

The connection between our sin and our ruined relationships is perhaps more obvious and less liable to speculation than cases of illness or other physical afflictions. If we needlessly explode in anger at our family, it should not surprise us when they eventually begin to put up walls against us. If we lash out at our co-workers or abuse our subordinates at work, we should count it as God's disciplinary action, rather than as a hardship in which we are the victim, when we lose our job. When we entrench ourselves in sin, we should not be surprised that, as it ruins us personally, it wrecks our ability to keep good relationships with others. Many of our damaged relationships have been the fallout and direct consequence of our sin.

God will at times afflict us to bring us to repentance. David opened this psalm seeking for relief from his affliction because God's discipline had made him realize the gravity of his sin. In Hebrews 12:7-11, we learn how God always aims this sort of hard discipline for our good:

> It is for discipline that you have to endure. God is treating you as sons. For what son is there whom his father does not discipline? If you are left without discipline, in which all have participated, then you are illegitimate children and not sons. Besides this, we have had earthly fathers who disciplined us and we respected them. Shall we not much more be subject to the Father of spirits and live? For they disciplined us for a short time as it seemed best to them, but he disciplines us for our good, that we may share his holiness. For the moment all discipline seems painful rather than pleasant, but later it yields the peaceful fruit of righteousness to those who have been trained by it.

God's fatherly care is such that He will not leave us entrenched in our sin. As we have emphasized, sin makes us miserable. Sometimes, God will let us have the full measure of that misery to show us how ruinous sin is. He disciplines us in that manner to turn us away from our misery-causing sin.

In the case of Psalm 38, David clearly perceived how his sin had caused his troubles. He helps us see that sometimes the reason that we suffer is because of our sin. He also helps us to see that God intends hard discipline to bring his people to repentance.

The Repentant Response

If David modeled how to acknowledge that his sin caused his troubles, he also modeled the proper response to our sin. He shows us that we should recognize when our guilt stands behind our suffering so that we turn away from our transgressions. We should be clear that the argument is *not* that every time we get sick or have relational difficulties it is necessarily because of our sin. The point is that when we see that our sin has caused our present troubles, we should not explain away why we are suffering. Instead, we should repent.

David modeled that response throughout Psalm 38. He did not mince words about what caused his trouble. His response teaches us that, in many situations, we should cease to ask, "God, why is this happening to me?" and instead start saying, "God, I'm sorry that I have sinned in this way so that you would so afflict me." David was direct in owning up to his sin and in not playing the victim when he knew that he was to blame.

We recognize that no magical link connects crime and affliction. David's sin could have had a very natural link to illness and hostility in ways that we considered in the earlier section. In the same way, if you lie about your taxes, it will cost you immense amounts of money. If you steal from others, you will go to jail. If you mistreat people, it will destroy your relationships. Sin often has obvious and, humanly speaking, natural rather than mystical consequences.

In this way, when you see the direct link between your sin and your misery, Psalm 38 instructs us that true repentance is honest about that connection. We take responsibility for the trial that we have brought upon ourselves. We easily look for reasons to explain away our misery without looking to our sin. We can easily act as though God has unexpectedly brought trouble upon us for no reason when we know full well why it is happening. We love to play the victim when we should really get to repenting.

This application means that we have to address tough topics in our own lives. Are things bad at home? Do you act like that difficulty is there because people change over time, and you don't know how to get along anymore? Or are you ready to admit your selfish refusal to engage well in those relationships? Are you denying that your actions may have actually created the very tensions you pretend are driving you away? We all must take responsibility for our part in living well with others.

What part of our trouble are we pretending is someone else's fault when we know the blame is really ours? What do we claim is due to someone else's shortcomings when we know that we missed the mark? Am I jealous of the praise others get, and so despise and badmouth them? Are we bitter because we feel that we don't get the treatment we want from our friends or even our church? There could be other reasons for all these repercussions, as germs were undoubtedly the natural cause of David's illness. Natural causes can go hand-in-hand with sin if you have engaged in sin connected to those natural reasons.

In Psalm 38, David shows us how to respond properly when we realize that our own sin has caused our own trouble. We need to rush to repent of our sin rather than point out the wrongs of others. Certainly, David could have pointed the finger at those enemies who were mounting against him. He takes another approach though. In verse 14, he puts the spotlight on his own deficiencies rather than on the wrong his foes are doing: "I have become like a man who does not hear, and in whose mouth are no rebukes." David's friends had become enemies, but since David knew that his sin had caused this chaos, he refrained from rebuking them.

In the previous chapter, one of our applications was to "lead" with repentance. We see now that Psalm 38 confirms that practical insight with concrete biblical grounding. When people wrong us, we should hold back from addressing their sin until we admit ours to them first. David exemplified the same principle of eagerness to repent which is embodied in the application of leading with repentance. He rushed to the Lord in admission of how his guilt had made a mess of his situation.

These reflections obviously pertain to the specific setting where we realize that our own sin is the reason for what has gone wrong in our lives. In other situations, things may go wrong in our relationships even when we are not the one who has sinned against another. In some cases, others will have sinned against you. Their sin may have caused the hardship in your life. These complications of living in a fallen world are why we need that measured and tempered approach to assessing how our own sin relates to our affliction. Nonetheless, we should always maintain the posture and practice of repentance. Our response to hardship should be self-awareness about when we sin; and when our difficulties are due to our own sin, they ought to bring us to explicit repentance.

Restoration in Light of Repentance

Now we can focus on how we can put David's pattern—that is, recognizing and reckoning with one's own sin—into practice. To embrace this application properly, we have to take the uncomfortable deep dive into the mire of repenting. We will run through some examples of what it means to confront our own sin and see how it means that, in those cases, we forfeit the right to see ourselves as victims of blind providence in our affliction.

We ought to resist the urge to blame our sin on someone else's shortcomings. Even if that factor may play into the situation at some point, we do better to emphasize our own need to repent rather than excusing our sin because of what someone else has done. For the man or woman committing adultery against your spouse—be that physically, emotionally, or even digitally—you do not get to say that the wreck of your marriage is because you did not get what you needed from your relationship. If you are a person who nags incessantly or who is distant, you do not get to say that it was because other people failed you. If you refuse to obey your parents, you do not get to say that it is because you struggle at school or with friends or whatever. If you wrong your friends, you do not get to say it was because you are struggling to get what you need from the world. Whatever our sin is in the situation, we must own it.

Rather than look for ways that we can blame our sin on someone else, we should repent and confess our sin without qualification. The only thing that we have the right to say is, like David, "I sinned; I confess my iniquity; I am sorry for my sin. I am wrong and I deserve all of God's arrows right into my heart and even worse." We may want to say more. We should resist that impulse until we have reckoned with the Lord for what we have done. We have to learn to run right into the full reality that our sins, wherever they fall in the spectrum of heinous, are all heinous.

Repentance is not the last word as if we stay forever brooding over how bad our sins have been. When we have gone to the Lord, and to others when appropriate, in repentance, then we ought to cry out like David in Psalm 38:21-22, "Do not forsake me, O LORD! O my God, be not far from me! Make haste to help me, O LORD, my salvation!" We call to God for mercy, not as if we deserve it or can force His hand into alleviating our situation, but because we know that we must cast ourselves into His grace. We should not leave ourselves in agony over our sin without seeking the Lord's reprieve, which He has promised to give us through the grace of Christ.

Our repentance does not obligate God to remove the earthly consequences from our sin even while He forgives us in the heavenly court. The thief who repents and finds everlasting forgiveness with the Lord may still have to serve prison time. We should not point fingers at God when He does not remove the earthly consequences of our sin but, like David in Psalm 38:6, "utterly bow down and prostrate; all the day go about mourning." In other words, we do not repent merely to get out of trouble. We repent because we know how heinous our rebellion against God's law is, and we long for restored relationship with Him. The reprieve that God has promised in Christ is not necessarily that the earthly consequences for our sin will magically disappear. We cannot be bitter when we must live with those repercussions.

Most importantly, only one reason explains why God can accept our repentance. We must cry to God not to forsake us *because of Christ*. Our repentance itself does not save us.

As Westminster Confession 15.3 says, "repentance be not to be rested in, as any satisfaction for sin, or any cause of pardon thereof." Jesus Christ alone saves us. The repentance that He works in us by the Spirit is fruit of that salvation, not its cause.

God sent Jesus Christ into this world so that God the Son might die in human nature to pay for all these crimes for which we must repent. In 2 Corinthians 5:21, Paul explained: "For our sake he made him to be sin who knew no sin, so that in him we might become the righteousness of God." Christ took our sin upon Him so that we might be credited as righteous. As He died on the cross because of your lawbreaking, He cried, "My God, my God, why have you forsaken me?" (Ps. 22:1; Mark 15:34). Jesus Christ was forsaken for your sake. He endured the penalty of God's wrath so that God might give you grace. No other place but the shelter of Christ's cross is firm enough to stand against the beating storms of our sin.

David's pattern also shows us the beauty of repenting as God's people. As 1 John 1:9 tells us, "If we confess our sin, God is faithful and just to forgive us our sin and to cleanse us from all unrighteousness." Christian, confess your sin boldly because Christ is boldly interceding for you to provide your forgiveness. We should stand confident in knowing that when we cry to God for mercy as we learn to hate our sin, God has made a promise to forgive. We can depend, not presumptuously but in faith, upon God's grace because it is guaranteed in Christ's blood. Our forgiveness cost the Father the life of His Son. How willingly God gave Christ out of love for you. How willingly then we should flee to Christ for rescue to find shelter in that love and find freedom from our sin and its curse.

Conclusion

Hardship may often befall us in the Christian life. In James 1:1-4, Scripture exhorts us about how to respond to those seasons: "Count it all joy, my brothers, when you meet trials of various kinds, for you know that the testing of your faith produces steadfastness. And let steadfastness have its full effect, that you may be perfect and complete, lacking in nothing." God does not let us slip into seasons of trial without purpose. He is using those seasons to bring our faith to deeper maturity, that we might be more fully rounded Christians.

Sometimes those trials may be for the purpose of bringing us to maturity as they prompt us to repentance. As we have seen, hardship in life may not be because of anything that we have done, and God may be using it in other ways to produce steadfastness in us. It may be the case, however, that God is using hardship to discipline us for how we have slipped into some serious sin or pattern of it. If we can identify a clear connection between sin and its consequence, we ought to let that discipline have its "full effect." We ought to turn from that sin and learn steadfastness against that particular temptation. As James implies in those verses, God's fatherly discipline in this way is for our good, because He always means it as a mark of His love to grow us into richer and stronger faith.

We began this chapter by thinking about buying fruit, especially about how the firmness of a fruit is supposed to be an indicator about its ripeness. Depending on how hard or tender our consciences are, we might struggle to let discipline have its full effect to bring about steadfastness in us. If we are too soft in our conscience, our over-sensitivity to correction might prevent us from learning from discipline. We might feel the force of disciplinary action but not be brought to repentance and greater maturity because we are so focused on feelings of disapproval that we avoid the issue itself. If we are too hard in our conscience, discipline may not have its full effect because we remain blind to how we need that correction. We do not see how we are wrong, assuming that the hardship we experience must be about something other than what we have done. A true understanding of repentance helps us tune our consciences to a proper firmness so that we become properly ripe for maturity in steadfastness in the Christian life.

Chapter Four

THE SELF-SEARCHING PSALMIST

Psalm 143

Life is super messy. It gets even messier when we think about real instances of sin and how repentance should come into play. In only rare situations where someone needs to repent is that need one-sided. Usually, sin moves with at least two-way traffic. When someone has sinned against us, we rightly want to see repentance from that person who has wronged us. At the same time, we likely still need to assess our own hearts concerning whether we have added our own sin to the situation too. Maybe that sin is against the person who sinned against us. Maybe it is exclusively before the Lord. Either way, even when we are the victim of someone else's sin, we might have our own sin to confess as well.

The balance of knowing our own responsibility before the Lord and knowing our need for His help is often hard to keep. Our tendency is to emphasize one side of the balance or the other often without much counterbalance. On the one hand, if we sense that we are the victim of someone else's sin, we often struggle to find any place to admit our own wrongdoing. To clarify that even further, we may not have any need as a victim to repent to the person who has wronged us. Still, we can struggle to admit any wrong on our part even only before the Lord Himself. Even then—especially in today's climate where we are having to reckon more deeply with victimhood—we might have difficulty in filtering this issue through the differing levels of how someone else may have wronged us. After all, my son leaving a small mess in my office, someone dangerously cutting me off on the freeway, and someone literally stabbing me in a parking lot are all very different degrees to which I might be a victim. On the other hand, victims who do have a sense of some wrong that they have committed can easily feel like they have no place to call to God (or to the church) for help. Neither perspective that emphasizes one side of this issue at the expense or exclusion of the other reflects a proper Christian approach to repentance.

The complexities that often surround instances of mutual or compounded sin create tensions and obstacles against a simple and always tidy set of applications. As this book has unpacked it thus far, this vision of a penitent people with deep and explicit repentance applies foremost to *so-called* everyday sin. This readiness to repent at a forthright level maps more easily onto the ordinary level of selfishness and mistreatment that we give one another on a daily basis. Even if it damages our pride, we should not find it overly difficult to regret and to apologize for being bitter at a family member who left a mess, did not help adequately around the house, or spoke without the kindness that we think they should have used. Sadly, petty faults such as these are not the only ways that we sin against one another.

Our experience in the Christian life is not limited to these normalities. I imagine that every reader will have at least known someone who has been either guilty or victim (or both) of more heinous sins. That raises difficult questions concerning repentance. If, as we saw in the previous chapter, our troubles can result from our sin, are we simply to endure silently through immense hardship under others' sin? Does the possibility of the Lord's discipline mean that I never speak up when someone seriously sins against me? On one hand, our call to personal repentance is unflinching. Whenever and however we are in the wrong, we should repent without writing off our sin because of what someone else has done. On the other hand, we must address a more complex side of repentance, which concerns *if and how* I should repent when, although seeing my wrongdoing, I have been the victim of someone else's sin. This problem is even more complex when perhaps the sin against me is in some way more serious than my own sin.

The gospel reality here is that Christ holds us close to Himself even when we struggle to repent. Even when we are hard pressed to recognize our transgressions and failures, believers are still the sheep that can never be snatched from Christ's hand (John 10:27-30). We are irrevocably His. Part of the gospel comfort we should have is that, when we are the victim, Christ sympathizes with us because He was the victim of heinous sin when those who hated Him flogged and crucified Him. When we are the one who wrongs someone else, although we need to repent, we can also be glad that Christ died to forgive those who wrong others. He even prayed for the forgiveness of those who victimized Him, "Father, forgive them, for they don't know what they are doing" (Luke 23:34). Undoubtedly, we often do not realize what we are doing to someone else. Thankfully, the gospel comes to bear for those who are victims, those who wrong others, and even those who can struggle to see where they fit among victims and wrongdoers. As, according to Westminster Shorter Catechism 87, repentance comes in light of apprehending the mercy of God to us in Christ, we must recognize then that repentant people are those who are in the hands of grace, helping us to work through our failures and how we have been failed.

Psalm 143 helps us contemplate repentance as we experience the harshest treatment from enemies, friends, and even family. This psalm is both David's expression of repentance and his cry for help in dire times, giving us a vivid picture of how we can hold those things together. Those who mistreated him were gravely wrong and were acting wickedly. Yet David also had to deal with his own sin. This chapter therefore argues that the posture and practice of true repentance does not preclude seeking relief from suffering. How we respond to sin and how we respond to suffering both matter—and they both ought to be biblically informed. This chapter is an encouragement to remember that we must seek God's help when we have been wronged *and* when we have done wrong.

The Situation

In contrast to many of the psalms, we don't have to guess as to what specific historical situation prompted David to write psalm 143. A very long tradition—including headings at the top of this psalm in the Greek translation of the Old Testament—suggests that the background is related to David's sin of adultery with Bathsheba and subsequent murder of her husband.

Scripture unfolds David's heinous actions in tragic fashion, while also giving us insight into how God responded to, as well as the consequences of, David's failure. In 2 Samuel 11, we have the account of David's sins where, from the palace roof, he spies a beautiful woman bathing. Although fuller considerations may apply in interpreting all the ramifications of how David sinned, he undoubtedly brought this woman Bathsheba, whom he knew to be Uriah's wife, to the palace with the intention of committing adultery with her. That straightforward aspect alone is enough to show David as grossly in the wrong.

David added to his sin though. When Bathsheba became pregnant after this event, David tried to cover it up by bringing Uriah—an honorable and dedicated soldier—home from the battlefield to spend time at home, so there would be a plausible occasion for why Bathsheba's child could be seen as her husband's. Feeling duty bound to his compatriots still at war, Uriah refused to sleep in a warm bed with his wife, foiling David's plan to cover up his sin. Although David aimed at a deceitful way out of being caught in his transgression, no such route was available.

David then intensified his sin even more. He sent Uriah back to the battlefield and gave a letter to Uriah for his commander, Joab. He instructed Joab to let Uriah lead the next charge on the battlefield with the extra detail that the other men should quickly pull back, leaving Uriah alone on the frontline. Despite Uriah's valiant loyalty to his fellow soldiers, David ordered them to abandon Uriah so that he might needlessly die on the battlefield. David murdered Uriah to cover up how he had already sinned against Uriah in committing adultery with his wife.

The story did not end with Uriah's death, since God still had plans to deal with David for his sin. In 2 Samuel 12, God sent Nathan the prophet to show David his sin. As Nathan confronted his king, God promised earthly curses upon David's life and family because of what he had done:

> "Now therefore the sword shall never depart from your house, because you have despised me and have taken the wife of Uriah the Hittite to be your wife." Thus says the LORD, "Behold, I will raise up evil against you out of your own house. And I will take your wives before your eyes and give them to your neighbor, and he shall lie with your wives in the sight of this sun. For you did it secretly, but I will do this thing before all Israel and before the sun." (2 Sam. 12:10-12)

The Lord would not simply let David's sin go. David would experience grave repercussions. That tragedy plays out as David's son upends the kingdom of Israel. In 2 Samuel 15–18, David's son Absalom turned against his father and wreaked havoc on the household. David fled Jerusalem and went on the run from his own son.

Psalm 143 is traditionally thought to be David's reflection about that time when he was on the run from Absalom. That context adds important aspects to understanding this psalm that ought to guide our thinking about repentance. The psalm has long been categorized as a psalm of repentance, which makes perfect sense against its historical background. The situation combined both David's need to see how his hardship was the fallout of his own transgression and his need for deliverance from those now sinning against him.

Hence, Psalm 143 sheds light on how we ought to hold repentance about our sin along with seeking the Lord's help when others sin against us. Even in David's opening line, he cried for mercy, followed with an acknowledgement that he was not righteous before God: "Hear my prayer, O Lord; give ear to my pleas for mercy! In your faithfulness answer me, in your righteousness! Enter not into judgment with your servant, for no one living is righteous before you" (Ps. 143:1-2). From the outset, David did not want God to assess him on his works, because he knew that he was sinful. As David wrote this psalm because of his experience of running from his murderous son, he acknowledged that his sin was at least involved in—and specifically the long-term cause of—that hardship. As he began Psalm 143, David repented of that sin again, knowing that he needed God's mercy for the transgressions that he had committed.

David's wrongdoing and the reality that people were wronging him stood together in this situation. David's sin was a contributing factor to this hardship when he was hunted by his own son. Nevertheless, he now was, on account of being wrongly hunted, himself the victim of evil. Despite the background of David's own sin, he now had enemies who were sinning against him: "For the enemy has pursued my soul; he has crushed my life to the ground; he has made me sit in darkness like those long dead. Therefore my spirit faints within me; my heart within me is appalled" (Ps. 143:3-4). In this psalm, David was able to hold together an understanding of the reality that he had sinned and needed to repent along with the reality that those who were now sinning against him also needed to repent. The victimizer had become the victim, and repentance was needed on all fronts.

The payoff from Psalm 143 is that everyone needs to repent of his or her own sin. If we have sinned against someone else, our sin does not give them an excuse to sin. They must repent of their wrongdoing just as we must of ours. If someone else has sinned against you, you cannot use that transgression against you as grounds for why you do not need to repent of any wrongdoing. Sin is always sin and requires repentance, whatever complicating factors may be swirling around it.

These reflections show us that the Bible has an equation for sin. That equation is not like algebra though. Sin on one side never cancels out sin on the other side. No sin can become a null set. Rather, the Bible's equation for sin is only multiplication. Sin compounds and adds to itself, but never nullifies another sin.[1]

Then, we should think about the even more complicated case of hardship ensuing from our sin. As Psalm 143 shows, sometimes I might have some blame in my own suffering, as David's past sin was the cause for his present affliction. Truly, our hardship may not always relate to something where we shoulder some of or all the guilt. Nevertheless, sometimes we have some blame in why we are in hardship. In the instances where we languish under how others are sinning against us, even if I have some blame in my suffering, it does not change the fact that evil things are happening to me and that evil people, or at least people behaving wickedly, are doing them. Even when we have reason to repent, it does not undermine that true evil has befallen us. The situation in Psalm 143 shows that we must learn commitment both to true repentance and to seeking the Lord's mercy in times of hardship. The situation was that real evil had come upon David and that he was still searching his own heart in the matter.

The Struggle

We hate relational complexity, especially concerning repentance. We love neat and tidy lines where we can analyze a

1 Thanks to Jonathan Cruse for this metaphor.

situation far enough to place blame on only one person. We love parsing situations down to their finest grain so that we can pinpoint the determining factor to say, "Well, you were that much more wrong than me, so I don't need to take responsibility for anything and it's all on you." Even for Psalm 143, many may have the impulse to interpret this situation one-sidedly so that David is either all to blame with no grounds to cry against someone else, or so that he did not truly have any reason to consider his own sin as he was the victim of attacks against him. The truth of the matter is that Scripture, even in David's own inspired assessment of his situation, does not give us the leeway to be that tidy.

We must reckon with that complexity in application to our own lives. We find ourselves in situations where even as we can say, "You shouldn't be doing this to me," we can still acknowledge, "Yes, I've done these things wrong," and repent of it. In many troubled moments between people, both sides need to repent. You might need help as the victim of sin and should certainly call out to God for that help. God will hear His people. That truth does not mean that we also do not have reasons to repent in the midst of that situation.

Given its complexities, David's situation obviously required some self-searching and personal wrestling. Even though David's sin was in a wider, broader sense responsible for his hardship, still David did not do anything *to Absalom* to deserve this sort of treatment from him. Even though David had sinned in the past, Absalom had no personal grounds for how he was treating his father. David had long since repented of those sins and had endeavored to live faithfully: "I remember the days of old; I meditate on all that you have done; I ponder the work of your hands. I stretch out my hands to you; my soul thirsts for you like a parched land" (Ps. 143:5-6). Despite David's prior repentance and new obedience, Absalom acted wrongly and evilly. Absalom needed to take responsibility for that sin.

On the other side of the equation, David's past sins did not require him to endure evil passively and silently, showing us that we should not indulge others' sin even as we repent of our own. To anticipate a potential question, the objection may come up that Jesus instructs us in Matthew 5:38-42 that we must turn the other cheek when wronged. Truly, we must heed and practice Jesus' teaching against retaliation. One consideration in wisely assessing what that enjoins upon us is to realize that a response to sin is different from a retaliation. We can *respond* as we experience evil, even if we do not have the remit to *retaliate*.

That distinction plays out in David's example. When Absalom sinned against him, David responded by fleeing and developing plans for how to retake his kingdom (Ps. 143:9). He consulted with friends about how they could help him by staying in Jerusalem (2 Sam. 15:24-29). At the same time, as he worked to overturn Absalom's sin of rebellion, he refused to retaliate against him. When it came time to act decisively, David ordered his commanders: "Deal gently for my sake with the young man Absalom" (2 Sam. 18:5). He did not want harm to befall Absalom despite all the sin involved. When Absalom was killed, David grieved immensely (2 Sam. 18:31-33).

David's example of responding without retaliation helps us see the proper way of applying Jesus' teaching specifically to help us wisely navigate our need to repent within a situation where we have been mistreated. Even as we endure evil, we still ought to hope for renewal and reconciliation. That outcome may not be possible, and our ability to work toward it in concrete ways might be very limited in some situations, but we still should hope and pray for it. Even as we go through situations of hardship, mistreatment, or trials of this sort where people are against us, we ought to hope—even if it seems unlikely, even if we do not know how to get there, even if there are no practical steps to take—for renewal and reconciliation. We ought to *hope* for it. We can hope for restoration even when we need to remove ourselves from certain evils against us. This obligation to hope for reconciliation is especially true when that evil is experienced in the context of close relationships that are important to maintain. Think David and Absalom. Absalom was both David's aggressor and David's son. David pleaded with the Lord that Absalom would cease being the former, but never the latter. He always wanted his son back.

Have you ever found yourself in a situation where it was hard to maintain this balance? When we are deeply hurt by someone close to us, the emotional scars left by their wrongdoing can easily lead us to feel vindictive and vengeful. If I were in David's shoes, I might easily grow to hate Absalom more deeply than a distant enemy precisely because he was supposed to be so close. This dynamic is why situations like pastoral abuse or mistreatment in the home are so difficult to overcome. The balance of taking action to prevent further harm to ourselves alongside a hope for true reconciliation is hard to maintain, but it is nonetheless a necessary tension as we traverse this fallen age.

Our response to sin against us cannot rest only with our plans at the human level. We need the Lord's help. We need Him to add His strength to our efforts so that we might find deliverance from our afflictions. David exemplified this awareness in Psalm 143:7-10:

> *Answer me quickly, O Lord*! My spirit fails! Hide not your face from me, lest I be like those who go down to the pit. Let me hear in the morning of your steadfast love, for in you I trust. Make me know the way I should go, for to you I lift up my soul. *Deliver me from my enemies, O Lord! I have fled to you for refuge.* Teach me to do your will, for you are my God! Let your good Spirit lead me on level ground!

This psalm then shows us how David rightly took himself to safety and cried also for God's rescue. He knew that his plans would come to nothing if the Lord did not help him. He even cried for the Lord to deliver him as he had already fled from danger.

David models something critical for our own prayer lives in that dependence upon the Lord. We might too easily think that we should pray until we have a solution planned. We accidentally slip into thinking that we pray until the Lord shows us a way forward, then the execution of that plan is up to us. In Psalm 143, as we have seen in the background of his escape from Jerusalem, David already had plans in place for how to navigate this horrible situation. He sought the Lord fervently to guide and to bless his way forward, nonetheless. We must cover every step of our road out of affliction and trial with earnest prayer, even when we think we see the way out.

One of our greatest needs for the Lord's help is perhaps strength and guidance to make godly decisions in the midst of hardest trials when we are the victim of sin. Within that stanza of Psalm 143:7-10, David wisely includes the petitions, "Make me know the way I should go, for to you I lift up my soul," and "Teach me to do your will, for you are my God! Let your good Spirit lead me on level ground!" Even though David knew that his opponents, who were in fact his own family, acted sinfully towards him and knew that he needed to remove himself from that situation and seek God's help against his enemies, he also knew that he was not totally beyond falling into sin himself and so called for God's help in making sanctified decisions.

From David's request for sanctified wisdom, we learn part of what it means to remain repentant, humble, and wise as we seek God's help for the way forward when we are the victim of serious sin. Despite how David was enduring heinous sin against him, he did not assume that everything he did would be correct. He did not use the affliction he endured as free license to do whatever he wanted. He did not think that his suffering through rampant sin from others' hands meant that he was excused for anything he had done or might do. David knew that he needed God to guide him to walk in accordance with God's law.

Psalm 143 instructs us to adopt the same approach when we are wronged. Like David, we look for ways to end our affliction and we seek the Lord to help us in that endeavor. Further, we should not assume that *any* way out of our trial is a righteous way. Rather, we must ask the Lord to help us make righteous decisions using sanctified wisdom. After all, murdering a manipulative and controlling boss is not the godly path out of tribulation at work.

We stay humble by not presuming that our experience as a victim means that we are now above sin ourselves. We stay repentant in knowing how easily we might stumble into sin on our part. We stay wise by pleading with the Lord to guide our steps forward in righteousness. As we seek the Lord to protect us and deliver us from whatever situation has made us a victim, we must remain on guard that we would not succumb to grave sin ourselves. May it never be that we would use our status as a victim in true need of the Lord's help to excuse our actions of victimizing someone else. We must love righteousness in all circumstances so that we would work to escape unrighteousness done to us and to avoid committing unrighteousness against others.

We also need, in that respect, to consider how biblical wisdom comes to bear in the Christian life. People often talk about discerning God's will as if it means certain knowledge of God's decree for concrete aspects of *our lives*. We want specific insight from above about what exactly to do about the situation before us, whether that be a decision about our career, a relationship, or even something more related to our topic of repentance. In contrast, the Bible most often speaks of seeking God's will as needing instruction and help in the very things that God has already revealed. God has already made known what His law is as He built it into creation (Rom. 1:18-32; 2:12-15), summarized it in the Ten Commandments (Exod. 20:1-17), and reexplained it in the new covenant Scriptures (e.g., James 1:19-25). Whereas we want God to tell us directly the next specific move to make, Scripture more pointedly emphasizes our need for God's help in applying the foundational principles that He has already made known to us.

We, following David's example, ought to pray for God's help in making sanctified decisions, not as if that means an expectation of new revelation but as if God will bring His inspired Word to bear upon our lives. As noble as it is to want divine help in the particulars of our own life, Scripture is infinitely more emphatic about our need for help simply in learning and keeping the foundational principles of God's law. David knew that reality and knew that, in troubled times, we need even more help to know and keep God's law.

The considerations in this section have shown that our struggle is often our need to respond rightly and well to wrong done to us in a practical way, while also seeking God concerning our proper spiritual response. The struggle is keeping together realities even when it might feel like they are in real tension. That tension might find expression in holding together how we need to repent of whatever sin we have done while also responding well to sin against us. It might also express itself in holding together the reality of knowing that we are the victim of sin with an awareness of our continual need to make sanctified decisions with God's help, that we might have His guidance in righteousness. The Christian life is full of complexities and tensions. The necessity for us to balance our own need to repent with how to respond to sins of others is only one of those intricacies, even if it is a very difficult one.

The Search

Our exploration of Psalm 143 so far has focused on how David reflected upon the complexities of his affliction to see how he wrestled with his own sin even amidst turmoil caused by others. Our next need is to reflect on more explicit application for how we should apply David's posture and practice of repentance to our own lives. In times when we are in turmoil and trouble, especially when it results from our own sin, we must admit our faults and acknowledge that we need God's forgiveness and guidance. We must always deal with our own sin before the Lord, even when that means doing so as others sin against us.

That application comes to bear concerning our need for the Lord's guidance to walk in holiness amid trial. We can so easily grow overconfident that we know what is right, leading us to trust our initial gut feelings about whether we are right or wrong in a given situation. By contrast, David knew that he still needed God's instruction and leading in holiness even while everyone around him seemed so obviously and blatantly in the wrong. He knew his own sin, and so he distrusted his own heart. We must search ourselves, and at least allow for the possibility that we need correction at some level or in some aspect. We should pursue deeper repentance, assuming that we have deceived ourselves in some way or another. That becomes difficult and complex when we face real world wickedness.

The upshot of our need to walk well before the Lord in whatever situation we might find ourselves, good or bad, is that, at the absolute bottom line, we are all still always responsible to deal with God for our own hearts and actions. Even when we recognize someone else's grievous transgressions against us, we must deal with the Lord for what we have done. That need does not mean we *only* repent, since we have seen that we might often have need to respond to sin against us in other ways as well. The space to respond to sin against us with *more* than our own repentance should still not squeeze out the place for our own repentance. Our sin is sin, even as we navigate it within the context of someone else's sin.

The hard reality is that sometimes we find ourselves in a situation where someone has sinned grievously against us, but we are also guilty of committing horrible sin against them. In such a situation, the complex truth is that both sides have committed inexcusable sin for which they need to repent. Action is needed in some measure to rebuke and correct both parties, so that both parties are defended in how they have been sinned against. Nevertheless, both should also bring outrage before God *against themselves* for what they each have done. We are all responsible for our own sin, even in the context of sin against us.

The Iliad's story of the Trojan war might offer some insight on this sort of complexity. Prince Paris of Troy seduces Helen, the wife of Spartan king, Menelaus, to leave her husband and flee with him to Troy. In retaliation, Menelaus gathers forces to attack the whole society of Troy—perhaps to reclaim his wife or perhaps using his wife as an excuse to siege a country that he had always wanted to conquer. Even the most heroic figure in the story, Prince Hector of Troy, fails to recognize Paris' awful sin and goes to war to defend his brother's adulterous actions. Achilles, the epic warrior, enters the battle mainly to slaughter and humiliate Hector for killing his dear friend. Who was the real sinner in this story? Perhaps we are on better ground to ask, were any of them at all in the right? Sin compounded upon sin as every character added to the accumulation of godlessness.

To add more complications in applying Psalm 143 to our own repentance, what about situations where the sides are not equally liable? I once saw a video interview of a married couple about how they pursued healing in their relationship. On the one hand, the husband confessed that he was addicted to illicit online material. On the other hand, this supposed minister then had his wife confess that she sinned by spending too much time with friends. The suggestion was that they were in mutually equal sinful struggles.

Without being privy to the more personal details of the situation, those sins on the surface do not seem as though they should have been equally categorized. This man subjected his wife to his unfaithfulness through his computer use, and he should confess and repent his heinous offense. Seemingly, he also ought to repent for gaslighting his wife by trying to nullify his sin because there were some minor improvements she could make in her attentiveness to their relationship. Perhaps she did have something to confess to God about her time with friends. Nevertheless, an inordinate amount of time given to a permissible and even good thing is not the same sort of sin as even a brief amount of time given to an outright violation of the seventh commandment.

Although it runs against the grain of some recent currents in broader evangelicalism that *in every way* reduce every sin down to the same level of offense, Christians have long understood Scripture to give us categories to recognize that not every sin is equal in every respect. Westminster Shorter Catechism 83 asks, "Are all transgressions of the law equally heinous?" and answers, "Some sins in themselves, and by reason of several aggravations, are more heinous in the sight of God than others." The two named factors to differentiate the heinousness of sin are "in themselves" and "by various aggravations." For the first factor, using the example from above, since adultery and lust are *in themselves* sinful, the husband's sin was more heinous than the wife's, since God's law does not prohibit time with friends. *Even if* the wife did truly spend an inordinate amount of time with friends, mistakenly losing track of time on one occasion is not the same thing as repeatedly disregarding time that should be spent at home. That one-time mistake should be easily overlooked, but the ongoing, conscious disrespect becomes heinous as it is willfully repeated as an example of "various aggravations." Not every sin is sinful in the same way, on the same level, or in the same respect.

That consideration qualifies how we consider our theme of repentance but does not undermine the truth that every sin requires repentance. We still affirm that every sin is deplorable before God and that sin of any sort or magnitude deserves everlasting condemnation (James 2:10). Certain categories, such as those outlined in Westminster Shorter Catechism 83, help us navigate situations, exemplified in Psalm 143, where we must search our own hearts even while dealing with someone else's sin against us. Still, the baseline point is that we need to place liability squarely upon the guilty party for their sin. *Whenever* we have true transgression, we ought to confess it. That repentance should not be offered as if it *automatically* means that we share blame for someone else's sin. We must all take personal responsibility for our actions and quit shoveling them off as if they are the product of communal or relational imperfections. We must all search ourselves for how we are responsible to repent before God.

Conclusion

Despite how Psalm 143 confronts us with difficult realities, it is also full of hope. As David closes his prayer, he records his final petitions: "For your name's sake, O LORD, preserve my life! In your righteousness bring my soul out of trouble! And in your steadfast love you will cut off my enemies, and you will destroy all the adversaries of my soul, for I am your servant" (Ps. 143:11-12). As we tie these verses into what we have already seen, we see that Psalm 143 has a straightforward, twofold connection to Christ.

The first connection is the baseline need to believe the gospel. David cries out for God to cut off his enemies. God will answer that prayer for us all, at least when Christ returns. He is coming to destroy His enemies and the enemies of His people (Rev. 19:11-21). That coming judgment summons us to believe the gospel because on our own we remain under that impending condemnation as God's enemies

(2 Thess. 1:5-12). We must all seek refuge in Jesus Christ as Savior or else we will be destroyed. On the cross, He was cut off in our place: by faith in Him, and only by faith in Him, we belong to Christ and are counted as having already been judged and crucified, as Christ died for us (Col. 2:11-15).

Second, for those cases where we might endure the hardship of sin against us, Psalm 143 points not only to Christ *for* us but also to Christ *with* us. As Christ suffered for us, He endured protracted hardship under the sin of other people who tortured and murdered Him. In all our hardest moments, Christ is never aloof from our pain. We have a great high priest who sympathizes with all our trials, who has endured trials and sufferings, yet without sin (Heb. 4:15). Psalm 143 is ultimately about Jesus who endured the affliction of others' sin so that He might rescue us. Jesus does not ask you to grit your teeth through pain. He comes to be with you, knowing the depths of your hurt but promising to walk with you in every moment of it.

Chapter Five

A REPENTANT COMMUNITY

Exodus 24

Food is amazing. Above and beyond its nourishing and tasty contributions, it also provides opportunity to mark great things in our lives. Throughout human history, people have marked and commemorated special occasions with food. Birthdays and weddings cannot go without cake. Graduations have to be followed by a nice meal. Anniversaries usually center around romantic dinners. Clearly, we use food to bind us together in celebration of important things.

God Himself also uses food to commemorate important things about His relationship with us, at times instituting meals to celebrate major events in His relationship with His people. Think how, even in the Garden of Eden, the tree of life was present so that Adam would have been able to eat its fruit if he had resisted the serpent's lie concerning the tree of knowledge of good and evil (Gen. 2:9; Gen. 3:22–23). In Isaiah 25:6-8, the Lord promised a celebration of coming redemption: "On this mountain the Lord of hosts will make for all peoples a feast of rich food, a feast of well-aged wine, of rich food full of marrow, of aged wine well refined … He will swallow up death forever; and the Lord GOD will wipe away tears from all faces, and the reproach of His people He will take away from all the earth, for the LORD has spoken." That promise of a celebration feast is renewed for us from the new covenant vantage in Revelation 19:9: "And the angel said to me, 'Write this: Blessed are those who are invited to the marriage supper of the Lamb.' And he said to me, 'These are the true words of God.'" God has repeatedly used meals as a way to deal with His people. More pointedly, during these meals, God is personally present to dine with His people.

One instance of those meals especially helps us grapple with how they might inform us about repentance in the Christian life. In Exodus 24, God hosted a meal to complete His covenanting with Israel at Sinai. Beginning back in Exodus 19, the children of Israel gathered at the foot of Mount Sinai where God addressed them, and they accepted the covenant in principle. Over the next several chapters, God explained the terms of this covenantal relationship. In Exodus 24, the people accepted those detailed terms. Upon that culmination, a ceremony occurred to mark the completion of this covenant. Of course, it included food.

We need to ask what this covenant meal means for us as we consider the doctrine of repentance. As these people gathered to commune with God, they all came with an equal need for forgiveness. The famous hymn, "The Church's One Foundation," expresses well how God's appointed meal marks the unity of God's people as we come together before God for grace:

> Elect from ev'ry nation, yet one o'er all the earth,
> Her charter of salvation one Lord, one faith, one birth;

one holy name that blesses, *partakes one holy food*,
and to one hope she presses, with ev'ry grace endued.[1]

The people in Exodus 24 all fully needed grace as they came before God. That means that none of them had pride of place as they assembled. Truly, the same is true for us when we gather around the Lord's table as the church. This chapter looks at this special meal in Exodus 24 to explore the main point that God's meals with His people—for us today being the Lord's Supper—function as a pledge of God's grace as well as an opportunity for our repentance.

Principles Pointing to Christ

Houses need a frame before plumbing, wiring, and walls can go in place. The same holds true with doctrine and application. To ensure that we have right application, clear theology needs to be laid out as a frame on which we can hang our applications. Accordingly, before we can apply the significance of the meal in Exodus 24, we should highlight several necessary doctrinal premises. Four doctrinal aspects deserve our attention, especially in how we can draw the lines explicitly from this passage's doctrines to their New Testament fulfillment. These four points with their New Testament fulfillment, which inform how we think about the Lord's Supper, help us link it with repentance.

Feasts of Fellowship

First, God celebrates His covenants with meals. The events of Exodus 24 are the highpoint in the account of God covenanting with Israel. The Mosaic covenant was an administration of the covenant of grace, meaning that believers during that period

1 Samuel J. Stone, "The Church's One Foundation," *Trinity Psalter Hymnal*, 404 (emphasis added).

were saved by grace alone through faith alone in Christ alone. Nevertheless, Moses' types and shadows emphasized the law to teach about how Christ would come to fulfill it and rescue us from its curse. In Exodus 19–24, God unrolls what this covenant means and requires, especially as it focuses on legal aspects.

The ceremonies in Exodus 24 ratified the covenant and marked the completion of God's formal relationship to make Israel a nation of his people. This culminating event itself culminates in verses 9-11 with a meal where God Himself was present: "Then Moses and Aaron, Nadab, and Abihu, and seventy of the elders of Israel went up, *and they saw the God of Israel.* There was under his feet as it were a pavement of sapphire stone, like the very heaven for clearness. And he did not lay his hand on the chief men of the people of Israel; *they beheld God, and ate and drank.*" This meal was special as a symbol that God had truly accepted them as His covenant people and was blessing them with His real presence.

Sometimes we have something like a ribbon cutting ceremony to mark the opening of a new building or a christening to celebrate the commissioning of a new ship. These events signify the official beginning of when we will begin to use these important things. This ceremony in Exodus 24 resembles that sort of inauguration. As the animals were cut for sacrifices, the ribbon was cut for the opening day of Israel officially serving as God's people, bound to Him in this covenant initiated at Sinai. The meal following that sacrificial rite was the celebration to commemorate the official commissioning of this people as God's covenantal nation.

We should draw the connection to our life in the new covenant. In that meal atop Mount Sinai, the elders alone went to the table, even though they did so as representatives of all the people. Our new covenant meal of the Lord's Supper is better because every professing believer receives the bread and the cup to dine with God. More crucially, God Himself was genuinely present at that covenant meal that confirmed His covenant with Israel. Whenever God's people eat an appointed covenant meal, then God is genuinely present. Truly, in general, God is always present everywhere. At these covenant meals, however, God is present in a special way to bless His people.

In the new covenant, Christ instituted the Lord's Supper for our spiritual nourishment. Just like that meal in Exodus 24, God is genuinely present at our table, namely as Christ is present with us in the meal. We can appeal to Exodus 24 again, since the food in that meal never changed into anything other that what it had been. Nevertheless, Scripture clearly affirms that God was present at that meal, since they saw Him. In the Lord's Supper, the bread and wine remain bread and wine, but Christ comes to be present with us in a special, spiritual way by His Holy Spirit.

Westminster Larger Catechism 170 helps us express this truth. It explains that "the body and blood of Christ are not corporally or carnally [that is, physically] present in, with, or under the bread and wine" but they "are spiritually present to the faith of the receiver." In this way, we should recognize that in the Supper believers "by faith…receive and apply unto themselves Christ crucified, and all the benefits of his death." Christ is present with us in the new covenant meal in a spiritual manner to bring His blessings home to us in a special way. Thus, we see how God's presence at the meal in Exodus 24 points to the extravagant spiritual reality of His special presence with His people in all His covenant meals.

Recognition of Reconciliation

Second, this sort of communion over a shared meal between God and His people rests upon an accepted sacrifice. In Exodus 24:4-8, Moses oversaw the process of offering sacrifices that ratified this covenant between God and Israel:

> And Moses wrote down all the words of the LORD. He rose early in the morning and *built an altar* at the foot of the mountain, and twelve pillars, according to the twelve tribes of Israel. And he sent young men of the people of Israel, *who offered burnt offerings and sacrificed peace offerings* of oxen to the LORD. And Moses took half of the blood and put it in basins, and half of the blood he threw against the altar. Then he took the Book of the Covenant and read it in the hearing of the people. And they said, "All that the LORD has spoken we will do, and we will be obedient." And Moses took the blood and threw it on the people and said, "Behold the blood of the covenant that the LORD has made with you in accordance with all these words."

The order within these events is important, as it shows the progress from offering a sacrifice to what it means for that sacrifice to be accepted. First, Moses oversaw the offering of sacrifices. Then, Moses put blood on the altar, indicating that this offering was put before God Himself. Next, Moses read the covenant book. Finally, Moses sprinkled blood on the people.

As we look to pull some significance from this order of events, we realize how the arrangement of steps symbolize the nature of being reconciled to God. Moses used the blood from the sacrificed animals to demonstrate the sort of relationship that this covenant conveyed to the people. He put blood on the altar *first* because that altar was the symbol of God's presence. As Moses put blood on the altar, which represented God's own presence, it indicated that God had accepted the sacrifice. Moses then read the covenant book, showing how God's Word is essential in our covenantal interactions with God, as it informs how we are to understand the significance of sacrifices, or anything else that occurs, as we encounter God. Moreover, God's Word carried the meaning of that sacrifice to the people, so that they would understand how to relate to God in light of it. As Moses lastly sprinkled blood on the people, it signified how the value of that sacrifice, which God had accepted, was applied to them. The full sweep of events highlights how an acceptable sacrifice grounds the communion between God and His covenant people.

This significance in the order of these events shows the pattern of how we receive forgiveness in Christ. In regard to the offering of a sacrifice, Christ the final high priest offered Himself as a sacrifice to procure forgiveness (Heb. 7:11-25). We know that His sacrifice was truly accepted as everlastingly effectual because He rose from the dead and ascended into heaven, showing that He and His work are accepted before God's own throne (Heb. 4:14-16). Like Moses reading the covenant book, the apostles command the reading and preaching of God's Word because, through that proclamation, God applies Christ's once-for-all sacrifice—which is truly effective to forgive sins—to people by drawing them to faith in Christ (1 Tim. 4:13; 2 Tim. 4:2; Rom. 10:13-17). As Moses sprinkled the sacrificial blood upon the covenant people, the sprinkled water of baptism seals the benefits of faith. Throughout Scripture, the act of sprinkling symbolically applies forgiveness and cleansing to people (Lev. 4:5-7; Num. 8:7; Ezek. 36:25; Heb. 9:15-23). So, the events in

Exodus 24 mean to instruct God's people today about how we relate to God on account of grace given in Jesus Christ.

That the events of Exodus 24 intend to teach us about Christ as the true basis of our covenant relationship to God prompts us to clarify how animal sacrifices worked in the Old Testament period. We must be clear that no one ever had a right relationship with God because of a mere animal sacrifice. In Exodus 24, the sacrificed animals did not effect any spiritual reality in themselves, since "it is impossible for the blood of bulls and goats to take away sins" (Heb. 10:4). Accordingly, Westminster Confession of Faith 8.6 helps us tackle what to make of those Old Testament sacrifices:

> Although the work of redemption was not actually wrought by Christ till after his incarnation, yet *the virtue, efficacy, and benefits thereof* were communicated to the elect, in all ages successively from the beginning of the world, *in and by those* promises, types, *and sacrifices*, wherein *he was revealed, and signified* to be the seed of the woman which should bruise the serpent's head; and the Lamb slain from the beginning of the world; being yesterday and today the same, and forever.

The main takeaway is that believers truly received the blessings of Christ's work—even before the Son came in His incarnation—as they learned about those benefits from the various features of their worship. More specifically, the animal sacrifices were a means to grant Christ's blessings to His Old Testament people, as those sacrifices symbolized His once-for-all sacrifice on the cross. The animal sacrifices did not themselves secure the forgiveness of sin or communion with God but taught God's people about how Christ's sacrifice would truly provide those saving blessings. Inasmuch as the true believers amid Israel understood what the sacrifice in Exodus 24 symbolized—namely, Christ's death for the ultimate forgiveness of sin—those sacrifices brought spiritual realities home to them.

Gifts can come wrapped in all sorts of different wrapping paper. My favorite wrapping paper at our house has some dancing penguins on it. For our purposes, the same gift can be delivered in any of those different wrappings. If I buy someone a set of drinking glasses, I can wrap them in my favorite penguin paper or in paper that has bears on it or in paper that has stars on it. If I'm running tight on time, I might even default to the super easy approach of dropping them in a gift bag. Regardless of the outer packaging, the same gift of drinking glasses is delivered.

The same is true throughout the different eras of the covenant of grace. During each covenant that God made with His people, the same gift was always at work even though the outward experience of the covenant appeared very different. Every covenant included ordinances—things that God commanded His people to do—that communicated Christ to believers. Christ and His saving benefits were always the gift wrapped inside each covenant. In the Mosaic covenant, animal sacrifices were a primary ordinance that taught people about Christ, especially concerning how Jesus would die to forgive the sins of everyone who believes in Him.

The symbolic value of the sacrifice in Exodus 24 as pointing to the true saving reality available in Jesus Christ brings the pattern of how we receive forgiveness in Christ to bear upon how we eat the Lord's Supper. Just as the animal sacrifice in Exodus 24 instructed God's people about Christ without itself being the basis of salvation, the bread and wine in the Lord's Supper teach us something about Christ's body and blood broken for us and apply spiritual realities to believers. Even with their real, spiritual, and symbolic connection to Christ, forgiveness does not come through mere eating the elements. That bread and wine, however, do confirm spiritual realities for us by teaching us that Christ's sacrifice has been forever truly accepted on our behalf, so that we can have fellowship with God at a covenantal meal.

The parallel underpinnings of Israel's meal with God and our Lord's Supper show the spiritual value of recognizing God's special presence with us at the Lord's Table. That process of sacrifice accomplished, accepted, and applied enabled God's people to eat that meal with God in Exodus 24. The same process of sacrifice accomplished, accepted, and applied enables people to eat the meal of the Lord's Supper with God. In this way, the Lord's Supper is only for believers, as entrance to this meal marks our profession of faith as we come for nourishment in light of having been forgiven. Moreover, our reception at the Lord's Table, wherein we trust that God is specially present with us in blessing, marks how our eating this meal confirms how we are in good fellowship with Him on the basis of Christ's once-for-all sacrifice.

A Meal with a Mediator

Third, the events in Exodus 24 teach us about our need for a mediator to approach God on our behalf. In Exodus 24:15-18, Moses alone could enter God's direct presence because Moses was the mediator of that covenant. He was the one who approached God on behalf of the people. Moses' role shows how only the mediator, the representative, can fully approach God. Although God came to be with the people on account of an acceptable sacrifice, only the mediator can go to God for the people.

In this case, Moses was a type of Christ, showing how we need the Savior to stand for us as we approach God. Only Christ has obtained the power to pass from earth to stand in God's very throne room, and He has done so as our high priest (Heb. 4:14-16). Although Moses' role signified Christ, ultimately "there is one God, and there is one mediator between God and men, the man Christ Jesus, who gave himself as a ransom for all, which is the testimony given at the proper time" (1 Tim. 2:5-6). Christ is the true Savior, standing as the mediator for all those who belong to Him by faith.

A Clearer Covenant

Fourth, the three ways that we have outlined culminate to prove that the new covenant is different and better than the old. In Exodus 24:3, "Moses came and told the people all the words of the LORD and all the rules. And all the people answered with one voice and said, 'All the words that the LORD has spoken we will do.'" God spoke the entire law to them as the terms of the covenant—and the people agreed to fulfill it!

If we do not think carefully, we might presume that the people's agreement indicated some sort of works righteousness. We might think that the way that they were supposed to maintain their spiritual relationship with God was their acceptance of all the rules. Even in the church's earliest centuries, however, Augustine, leading the charge for God's grace against legalism, helpfully explained how instances like this one are meant to lead us all to Christ. According to Augustine, in the old covenant "given on Mount Sinai, only earthly happiness is expressly promised…the land of promise [with] peace and royal power...are the promises of the Old Testament. And these, indeed, are symbols of the spiritual blessings which pertain to the New Testament."[2] In other words, the Mosaic covenant served a teaching role in redemptive history to show us how we need the Savior. Just as we saw above from Westminster Confession 8.6, Augustine helps us understand the truth that, by faith, believers under the old covenant received Christ in advance, like we do. As Hebrews 4:2 explains about the old covenant people who died in the wilderness, "good news came to us just as to them, but the message they heard did not benefit them, because they were not united by faith with those who listened." Strikingly, the good news—the gospel!—went to God's old covenant people *just as* it comes to us in the new covenant. God always had the same gospel of salvation in Jesus Christ for His people who would have faith in Him and be joined to those who receive the blessings of that message. The outward features of the old covenant, which may strike us as focused heavily on their works, intended to teach all God's people about spiritual realities that become clearest in the new covenant.

Those lessons focused on teaching about the effects and curse of sin as well as about how Christ has fulfilled the whole law for us. In Galatians 3, Paul reminds us that the law never allowed for some form of our works righteousness to save us. Rather, the law had a teaching role for God's people. This old covenant was a guardian to show us that we cannot earn blessings by works, so we must be justified by faith (Gal. 3:23-26). God imposed those demands upon Israel,

---

2 Augustine, "On the Proceedings of Pelagius," §14, in Philip Schaff (ed.), *Nicene and Post-Nicene Fathers, Series 1*, 14 vol. (Christian Literature Company, 1887), 5:189.

specifically so that, when they failed, they would know that they could obtain heavenly blessings only by faith. The new covenant is better than the old because the old pointed to earthly, symbolic blessings and said, "you must do," but the new points to heaven itself saying, "Christ has done." Salvation has always been by faith alone in the Messiah, and this function of the law under Moses showed how sinners have a desperate need for the Savior.

The four premises pointing to Christ (the feast of fellowship, recognition of reconciliation, a meal with a mediator, and a clearer covenant) all teach that we can have communion with God only because of Christ's saving work.

A Prodding to Peace

With a fuller understanding of how God is present at special meals with His people in place, we can connect it to our topic of repentance. Since it was a sacrifice that opened the door for God's people to come to that meal in Exodus, we realize that we come to our meal with God as people in need of forgiveness. Our condition should also remind us that we are all struggling sinners who should be gracious with one another.

Do you know a fellow church member who happens to drive you bonkers? People can do all sorts of things that irritate us. It makes me slightly anxious that I don't have someone in church who flat drives me mad because it causes me to wonder if I'm the one making everyone crazy!

As we participate in the life of our church, we can easily get super frustrated with our brothers and sisters when not everything goes as we prefer. So many reasons abound that we can fall into this trap. We sometimes get bothered with people who approach things differently than we do or who emphasize different things. Sometimes we get latched onto our own particular concerns. Sometimes we see things that we think genuinely need to be better. Sometimes we have personality clashes. Sometimes we see that others are stuck in real sin. Sometimes we ourselves are stuck in sin and look for ways to blame someone else. Divisions in the church are always a clear and present danger.

The events of Exodus 24 should have a profound leveling effect in making us see why we ought to be long-suffering and abundantly gracious with one another. Strikingly, *everyone* who gathered to mark this covenant with God, which was followed by the meal, had to be covered with blood. They *all* needed forgiveness. They *all* also came acknowledging their sinfulness. They were repentant as a people, coming in unison to receive forgiveness and to commune with God.

When we gather for the Lord's Supper, let us realize that we too must come to the table in repentance. On the one hand, some in the Reformed tradition have at times turned the necessity of examining ourselves for the table into an overly intense emotional introspection. That overemphasis misses the mark because we should not turn our need to come penitently into a way of earning our seat at God's table. It is not as if we deserve to be there on account of feeling bad enough about ourselves. On the other hand, we should not write off the true need for repentance that the Lord's Supper highlights for us. The right balance will help us.

Westminster Shorter Catechism 88 calls the Lord's Supper an *ordinary* means that Christ uses to communicate the benefits of redemption to believers. We should also not forget one of our guiding points, that the catechism says that repentance is a saving *grace*, meaning it is a gift that God works in His people. So, if repentance accompanies the ordinary means of grace, repentance should be *ordinary*. To be clear, the ordinariness of repentance does not mean that it should be lackluster—rather, it means that it should be a regular and standard feature of the Christian life.

I am an avid coffee drinker. Ever since I made my way through seminary by working at a coffee shop, it has been part of my daily routine. Whatever you might think of me for having a dependence on it—but I guess a book on repentance is the place to admit such an inadequacy!—I become acutely aware when I have gone without coffee for more than a day or so. How so? The dreaded caffeine headache that is more splitting than any other kind of headache that I get. It is a physiological signal demanding what my body craves as part of its routine and regular maintenance.

This anecdote shows how ordinary parts of our life are important. Coffee is a daily part of my life that really jams up my performance when missing. So, as we consider repentance as an *ordinary* feature of life, accompanying the ordinary means of grace, its ordinariness does not suggest that it is lackluster or menial. Rather, its ordinariness indicates how essential it is. We should feel it if repentance has gone missing from our lives. We should feel pains akin to a caffeine headache—repentance is far more critical than a caffeine fix! We should have an addiction to repentance that leaves a mark when it goes missing. Repentance, as an ordinary and regular staple of the Christian life, helps keeps us in order and functioning well.

A church marked by the regularity of repentance proves itself to be, not a museum of saints, but a hospital for sinners. One hymn about the Lord's Supper well captures this sentiment for approaching the table in repentance:

Wilt thou own the gift I bring?
All my penitence I give thee;
thou are my exalted King,
of thy matchless love forgive me.[3]

Because we all come to the table knowing that we need Christ to receive our repentance there, we should come to the Lord's Supper realizing that all faithful Christians are doing the best that they can. So, even if someone bothers you, the reason that they are acting so off key and that they might be unable to admit their faults or foibles, might be that that they are afraid of how others will receive them upon owning up to their shortcomings. The church needs to be a place where people find gracious help to grow in their repentance.

That responsibility we have in the church points to a great biblical truth that pertains to our relationship to one another in helping each other in repentance. Instead of eagerly pouncing on imperfections and annoyances, or instead of letting our bitterness simmer, we remember Galatians 6:1-2: "Brothers, if anyone is caught in any transgression, you who are spiritual should restore him in a spirit of gentleness. Keep watch on yourself, lest you too be tempted. Bear one another's burdens, and so fulfill the law of Christ." Note, the context of our instruction to "bear one another's burdens" is "if anyone is caught in any transgression." If we think that someone is not only bothersome but even stuck in sin, we are supposed to help them. We should come alongside them to help them repent. All the while, we must keep watch on ourselves by maintaining the posture and practice of repentance so that we do not also fall prey to temptation.

---

3 Greek hymn, "Let Thy Blood in Mercy Poured," trans. John Brownlie, *Trinity Psalter Hymnal*, 198.

Repentance must be a key aspect to the culture of any congregation, in part because it helps preserve and propagate the peace and unity of the church. People who are genuinely repentant of their own sins should have the characteristic of being slow to anger with their fellow Christians who may well be struggling. The Lord's Supper includes a prodding to remember that we all gather as people who need grace and forgiveness, so we should not only look to God for mercy but look to our table mates to extend mercy. That prodding is part of God's gracious provision to keep peace among His people.

Conclusion

Our closing reflection in this chapter should crystallize how the Lord's Supper is a meal wherein God comes to nourish and commune with forgiven sinners. In Exodus 24, we saw the two truths that the people needed to be covered in blood to remove their sins, and that God was specially present in communion with them through a covenant meal. The application for us is that God still extends the promises of forgiveness and communion.

We can see that application when we recognize how sacrifices and meals in the old covenant differ from how the new covenant works. In addition to the demand for repeated sacrifices of bulls, goats, and lambs, especially the Passover emphasized the need for a sacrificed lamb (Exod. 12:1-13). Critically, we often connect our Lord's Supper with the Passover that centered around a sacrificed lamb made into a meal (1 Cor. 5:7). That connection helps us understand profound realities about the Lord's Supper.

The difference between the old covenant Passover and the new covenant Lord's Supper comes to bear on this application. As we approach the Lord's Supper, we need to remember not only what *is* on the table, but also what *is not* on it. Have you ever thought about how, at our new covenant Passover, no lamb is on our table? In the old covenant, the repeated sacrifices were needed because that yearly lamb never forgave sin in itself. We have bread on our table, but no lamb, because our true lamb is the One who died once-and-for-all to deal definitively with sin and who stands forever in heaven to apply His effective sacrifice. Thus, as He instituted the Lord's Supper, Jesus also said, "This cup that is poured out for you *is the new covenant* in my blood" (Luke 22:20). Our table holds only bread and wine because the Lamb of God has definitively dealt with our sins.

At the Lord's table, we ought to give thanks that no lamb is served. The true lamb, Jesus Christ, entered history to die for our sins, pouring out His blood on the cross to put an end to our transgressions. Jesus Christ offers us forgiveness if we take hold of Him by faith. For those who trust in Jesus, God has accepted Christ's death instead of yours to satisfy His justice, and now God accepts you as righteous in His sight.

For those whom God has forgiven in Christ, Christ also promises communion. Christ is genuinely present, not in a physical manner as if these elements turn into Him, but in a spiritual manner: "The cup of blessing that we bless, is it not a participation in the blood of Christ? The bread that we break, is it not a participation in the body of Christ?" (1 Cor. 10:16). We truly receive Christ for our spiritual nourishment if we come to the Supper trusting Him for new life.

For this reason, God's Word should be read and preached in such a way as to lead sinners to Christ time and again so that we might find joy in our salvation. To that end, the sermon should also aim to bring repentant sinners to the Lord's Supper well. As he exhorted seminary students, Geerhardus Vos drew this connection in reminding preachers to keep in mind that the sermon should align clearly with receiving the sacrament:

> A good test to apply is the frequent comparison of the purport of your sermon with the purport of the sacrament. The word and the sacrament as the means of grace belong together: they are two sides of the same divinely instituted instrumentality. While addressing themselves to different organs of perception, they are intended to bear the identical message of the grace of God – to interpret and mutually enforce one another.[4]

God's Word proclaimed should bring the message of God's grace home in such a way as to bring home the celebratory implications of being invited to the Lord's Supper. As professing believers walk to the table, God uses that meal to help us walk away from our sin.

We must remember that the new covenant meal is for sinners. It is for those who need forgiveness. We rejoice to repent at Christ's table, for this bread and this cup point us *upward* to God as He seals the promise of forgiveness. We also come repentantly looking *to each side*, knowing that all who receive this meal come needing help to live faithfully to Christ. We come as a family, sometimes strong but often struggling. So, let us repent together, helping each other to this meal, knowing that even if we limp, we limp towards our beautiful Savior who has done everything to feed us with everlasting life.

---

4 Geerhardus Vos, "The Gracious Provision," in *Grace and Glory: Sermons Preached at Princeton Seminary*, new ed. (The Banner of Truth Trust, 2020), 251.

Chapter Six

FRUITS IN KEEPING WITH REPENTANCE

Luke 3:1-9

Sticking out like a sore thumb is hardly ever a good thing. If you went to a football game, you would be shocked to see your team marching onto the field with one of the players carrying a hockey stick. That player would obviously be out of place. You know that football players are supposed to be prepared for football, not for hockey. The fact that this player carries a hockey stick shows him out of accord with what football is supposed to be like. He is out of step not only with the expectations, but even with what this community is supposed to be doing.

We ought to be just as shocked if we look at the church and find that someone is not characterized by repentance. Earlier, we considered the first of Martin Luther's Ninety-Five Theses where he reminded us that, "When our Lord and Master Jesus Christ said, 'Repent,' he willed the entire life of believers to be one of repentance."[1] His point was

1 Martin Luther, "The Ninety-Five Theses," 41.

that repentance is a permanent, essential, and prominent aspect of what it means to live the Christian life. Repentance should be a fixed posture and practice for every Christian throughout their entire walk with Christ. If a Christian lacks repentance, he or she should stick out like a sore thumb.

Throughout these studies, we have looked at various aspects of the doctrine of repentance and what it means to be a penitent people. Westminster Shorter Catechism 87 explains that "Repentance unto life is a saving grace, whereby a sinner, out of a true sense of his sin, and apprehension of the mercy of God in Christ, does, with grief and hatred of his sin, turn from it unto God, with full purpose of, and endeavor after, new obedience." This description captures how repentance means turning away from sin and striving for new obedience. Both aspects are crucial and both take serious consideration of our own hearts. Most importantly, that striving for new obedience is because our repentance has been a turning *unto God* with a sense of His mercy in Christ. To reject sinful desires and to chase after the ways that God would have us live is simply part of the recognition that God has good things to offer His people.

In addition to the main facets of repentance that we have brought home for our personal application, we also need to take account of how our doctrine of repentance should shape the culture of our whole church. Christians should be a penitent people both at the individual level and holistically when considered as a body of God's people. This chapter highlights from Luke 3:1-9 that the Scripture enjoins upon God's people that repentance characterize our rank. Just as the football player with a hockey stick would be immensely out of place on the football field, so too a Christian without repentance is out of place in the church—or at least he or she *should* be. Thus, our main point in this chapter is that God's covenant community is directed to overt and explicit repentance.

Obvious Repentance

Repentance easily falls into the backdrop of the Christian life. All Christians will acknowledge in a blanket fashion that they are imperfect and need to repent. Every biblical church will affirm that it is full of people who sin and need forgiveness. Ought this truth to operate merely behind the scenes of our church life though?

John the Baptist shows us how repentance is supposed to be a prominent feature of God's covenant community. He had a special role in biblical history as he prepared the way for Christ's ministry, including how he called God's covenant people to practice overt repentance. Rather than limiting his admonition for repentance to unbelievers and the patently ungodly, John addressed those who were in good standing among God's people. As we will see, John's summons to God's people to repent teaches the church about how we must be a community that is marked by true, real, and obvious repentance.

In Luke 3:1-9, we learn about the beginning of John's ministry, with a spotlight on a few features that help us understand how his call to repentance has abiding relevance for Christians today. The initial information in verses 1-2 simply situates these events in relation to precise historical reference points. More pointedly for our purposes, although we have met John the Baptist earlier in Luke's Gospel, Luke 3:3 gives the first summary statement of what John's ministry was about: "And he went into all the region around the Jordan, proclaiming a baptism of repentance for the forgiveness of sins." John's ministry paved the way for Christ's ministry by focusing on the people's need for repentance.

John's role was special because he occupied a transitional spot in God's saving plan. Technically speaking, even though he appears in the New Testament, John was the final old covenant prophet. Despite his appearance directly before Christ came onto the public scene, he culminated the old covenant prophets, namely, by pointing to the Messiah's arrival. Hence, in Luke 3:4-5, the prophecy from Isaiah 40:3-5 is applied to John's ministry: "As it is written in the book of the words of Isaiah the prophet, "The voice of one crying in the wilderness: 'Prepare the way of the LORD, make his paths straight. Every valley shall be filled, and every mountain and hill shall be made low, and the crooked shall become straight, and the rough places shall become level ways, and all flesh shall see the salvation of God.'" Isaiah foretold one who would minister in the wilderness as the messenger, paving the way for God's coming.

John's work reinvigorated the message that sinners need to repent and be rescued from the consequence of their sins. This announcement helped prepare the way for Christ's coming by reminding God's people of how sinful they were and how they needed a Savior. In verse 7, John brought a hard rebuke to his hearers, pulling no punch in how he addressed them in their sin: "He said therefore to the crowds that came out to be baptized by him, 'You brood of vipers! Who warned you to flee from the wrath to come?'" They needed to hear that they were wicked, and that God's wrath falls upon wicked people.

Although this whole context shows that John's ministry had a direct relation to the need for the people's repentance, the material most directly relevant for our reflections appears in verse 3 and verse 8, where John was "proclaiming a baptism of repentance for the forgiveness of sins," and exhorting the people to "Bear fruits in keeping with repentance." John called for direct action to live repentantly before God as His people.

Although often overlooked, we ought to take careful note that John's baptism was not *Christian* baptism like the baptism we receive as the mark of entry into the church. John was baptizing prior to when Christ instituted our baptism, and we have no evidence that He was using the necessary formula of baptizing in the name of the triune God (Matt. 28:19). Our Christian sacraments of baptism and the Lord's Supper were instituted personally by Christ, which He did not do for baptism until after His resurrection.

The record of Paul's initial ministry in Ephesus confirms that John's baptism was another sort of baptism than we receive. In Acts 19:1-5, Paul found a rather surprising situation where some disciples had seriously deficient understanding of who God is as well as a need for Christian baptism.

> And it happened that while Apollos was at Corinth, Paul passed through the inland country and came to Ephesus. There he found some disciples. And he said to them, "Did you receive the Holy Spirit when you believed?" And they said, "No, we have not even heard that there is a Holy Spirit." And he said, "Into what then were you baptized?" They said, "Into John's baptism." And Paul said, "John baptized with the baptism of repentance, telling the people to believe in the one who was to come after him, that is, Jesus." On hearing this, they were baptized in the name of the Lord Jesus."

These disciples had been instructed in John's message and had been baptized according to John's baptism, but they lacked some important updates that had come as people learned truly who Christ is. They were unaware that the Holy Spirit was even a divine person! Their lack of knowledge of that crucial point confirms that John's baptism, which they had received, was not applied using the name of the triune God, including the Spirit. These disciples, therefore, now had to receive baptism into Christ, using the triune God's name.

John's baptism served another purpose than to enroll people as disciples in the church community. John's baptism was different than Christian baptism as we know it. Because John's baptism served a different purpose than to bring people into the covenant community, it provides no warrant to explain Christian baptism as a profession of personal repentance. When we recognize how John's baptism differs from ours in this way, we can then understand its profound significance in teaching us about our repentance as members of the church: John's baptism was not an initiation rite into the covenant community but was directed towards those who were officially already part of the covenant.[2]

As directed toward those who were already members of God's people, John's baptism was a reaffirmation of commitment to God and public acknowledgement that members of God's covenant saw their ongoing need for repentance. John's baptism was a ritual that demanded God's people to consider their sin.[3] This baptism shows that because the people of Israel were externally members of the covenant community, they still had to have a proper response to God. They could not depend on the fact that

2 Darrell L. Bock, *Luke*, 2 vol. (Baker Books, 1994), 1:289.

3 Bock, *Luke*, 1:289.

they were within God's people in an official manner, as John himself addressed in verse 8: "And do not begin to say to yourselves, 'We have Abraham as our father.' For I tell you, God is able from these stones to raise up children for Abraham." The status of membership in God's covenant did not excuse anyone from the need for true faith and true repentance. Mere external religion was never acceptable among God's people.

We gather from these reflections that God's people, as the covenant community, ought to have acknowledgement of their need to repent. In Luke 3:1-9, we see that this baptism summoned God's people who live within the covenant community to ongoing, forthright, and explicit repentance. John's baptism summoned believers to make their repentance explicit and obvious. God's people were called to show their repentance, and they did. That public act from John's ministry helps us understand more deeply why churches today often devote a portion of their worship services to the confession of sin. That time of reading God's law, perhaps accompanied by brief reflection on how the Scripture passage should move us to repentance, followed by a churchly prayer of confession, is a rich way that the new covenant community today embraces the same summons that God's covenant people received from John the Baptist. In whatever manner they do so, God's people together rightly acknowledge their sin before the Lord and their need for His mercy in an obvious way.

Uniforms help show how certain people belong together. Sports teams wear uniforms to identify themselves as playing for a certain side in the game. Workers wear uniforms to display why they are on site and whose purpose they embody. Christians ought to have a "uniform" of repentance as one way to show the world that they are playing on the same team and working for the same cause. As the people of God, they ought to have repentance as an obvious marker that binds them together.

Our Repentance

How do we more clearly work out how to apply what we learned about John's baptism as differing from baptism into Christ as the mark of entry into the church? While our baptism into Christ seals God's promises in the covenant of grace, John's baptism was a conscious exercise in professing repentance *within* God's community. John, since "he went into all the region around the Jordan," spoke to those who were already initiated into God's covenant. His hearers were circumcised members of Israel. They and their children had received the Old Testament equivalent of baptism into God's Old Testament church. Most pointedly, they still had to repent of their sins.

That call for God's people to repent links directly to relevant application for our own lives. Most readers of this book will likely be baptized members in Christ's church. If you are in a Baptist church, that means that you have made a public profession of faith. If you are in a Reformed or Presbyterian congregation, like the one where I serve, you and your children have been incorporated into the community where God distributes His saving blessings through His means of grace.[4] Either way you understand it, in baptism, God places us into His covenant. All of us agree (at least we should!) that receiving this sign of entry on its own is not enough.

4 Reformed theology has traditionally referred to this relation as belonging to the external administration of the covenant. For a more detailed treatment of this idea, see Harrison Perkins, *Reformed Covenant Theology: A Systematic Introduction* (Lexham Academic, 2024), 273-300.

We cannot depend on church membership alone, but we must wholly and truly rely on Christ's merits for our standing with God. As part of the church, we must truly place our faith in Christ Jesus for salvation.

This observation brings us to the heart of considering the church as a penitent people. It tells us that repentance is an ongoing and continual need for every one of us. Proper Christian baptism happens once and initiates us into the church. The act of repentance, however, needs to happen repeatedly throughout the Christian life. One hymn captures this mindset as it ought to belong to the whole church:

> Kind and merciful God, we have sinned in your sight,
> we all wandered far from your way;
> we have followed our desire,
> we have failed to aspire
> to the virtue we ought to display.[5]

This song highlights the "we" dimension of repentance. It marks how repentance is a practice for the singular voice and for the plurality. The church as a corporate people needs awareness of our sin and how we have come short of who we ought to be. As repentance should characterize the church, it must be an ongoing and continual practice.

Repentance is commonly acknowledged as belonging to our conversion. Some traditions place a heavy emphasis upon our conversion as including an experiential crisis of recognizing our great sinfulness at a general and specific level. Although it is beautiful when God saves people out of a horrifically godless life, an overemphasis on that sort of crisis experience of repentance might make it easy to link

---

5 Bryan Jeffery Leech, "Kind and Merciful God, We Have Sinned," in *Trinity Psalter Hymnal*, 180.

repentance merely to the beginning of the Christian life. It might suggest that the real form of repentance is one of great tumult in turning away from sin rather than a regular posture and practice of repentance before the Lord throughout the Christian life. A wrong outlook on how repentance works at the beginning of the Christian life might obscure how it works throughout the duration of the Christian life.

The nature of repentance as an ongoing necessity in the Christian life indicates why we must situate it properly in the scope of salvation. Because repentance must be an unceasing feature of the Christian life, it must belong to the process of sanctification. John Colquhoun explained: "Repentance, therefore, is the constant exercise of the true Christian as long as he is in the world. He will not leave off repenting till he perfectly leaves off sinning."[6] Hence, repentance "must always be the sinner's duty."[7] Because repentance is the ongoing responsibility of the Christian, it must come after justification. Repentance cannot be a condition for justification because we can never repent adequately to put it behind us. We cannot tuck repentance on the front side of justification as if, supposedly having repented unto justification, we have an excuse to ignore it thenceforth as a fulfilled condition behind us.[8]

Repentance fits into the Christian life like the difference between surgery and dialysis. If it goes well, surgery takes place once and for all with a successful result. In that respect, regeneration and justification are both like surgery. God does them in a complete way once and for all. On the other hand, sanctification and repentance are like dialysis. They

6 Colquhoun, *Repentance*, 104.

7 Colquhoun, *Repentance*, 148.

8 Colquhoun, *Repentance*, 147–74.

have to keep happening to keep things going in the right direction. Repentance is a facet of sanctification whereby we keep turning away from sin.

Because, as we considered in our first chapter, sanctification is one of Christ's twofold benefits, we know that it bears an intimate connection to our relationship with Christ. Sanctification is one expression of our union with Christ. It is a gift to those who are made right with God. As Colquhoun put it, "Every man who is justified is *entitled to sanctification*, of which the habit and exercise of true repentance are essential parts. A pardoned sinner, then, cannot but exercise, and advance in the exercise of evangelical repentance."[9] While our sanctification is ongoing, we know that Christ is with us, working upon us and staying near to us. Sanctification's ongoing nature means that sin will always be close at hand in this life. Because its ongoing nature is a benefit of Christ, it also means that Christ will also always be close at hand in this life. If, this side of glory, we will never be rid of sin at least we know that sanctification means that we will never be rid of Christ either. Christ is always near to His people because He continually sanctifies those whom He has clothed with His righteousness.

We ought to make sure to adopt the view of repentance as an ongoing, regular, and ordinary feature of living out our faith. The approach of a general acknowledgement of a need to repent while nonetheless keeping it in the backdrop, and the approach of limiting our experience of repentance to merely the beginning of the Christian life, are both inadequate in emphasizing repentance and our need constantly to turn away from sin and back to Christ. For these reasons, Westminster Confession of Faith 15.5 says

9 Colquhoun, *Repentance*, 165.

that "Men ought not to content themselves with a general repentance, but it is every man's duty to endeavor to *repent of his particular sins, particularly*." We have an obligation to keep ourselves continually on our knees before the Lord in repentance.

Let's spell out this application further. Certainly, we will never search ourselves thoroughly enough to know every sin we commit, and the Confession does not mean to send us into a never-ending introspective spiral. Of course, we have a need for general repentance as well. As Chad Van Dixhoorn explains about the situations addressed in the confession, "The problem is that their repentance is *always* general."[10] The exercise of recognizing and naming our specific sins in repentance before the Lord is not meant to make us think that we can ever repent thoroughly enough. The purpose is that we would realize our need to turn away from sin in a real and specific way, so that we can leave it with Christ and grow in greater ability to serve Him. The beautiful thing is that the more specific sins we confess to Christ, the more specific instances we have when we see His great love for us in forgiving those sins.

These considerations confront us with the inadequacy of reductionist approaches to repentance. Although we should not diminish the great value of belonging to the church and attending to the ordinary means of grace, we cannot rest upon our mere presence in the church for security before God. The position of being a member "in good standing" of a local church—which means that our leaders have not found anything in our lives that calls for corrective church discipline—is a great blessing that ought to bring

10 Chad Van Dixhoorn, *Confessing the Faith: A Reader's Guide to the Westminster Confession of Faith* (The Banner of Truth Trust, 2014), 200 (italics original).

serious comfort to souls who are frequently troubled with wondering if they have repented enough before the Lord.[11] That comfort for troubled souls should not be used as a way to wave off our obligation to examine ourselves. Further, although we should never overlook self-aware repentance as one element of a credible profession of faith to become a communicant member of a church, we cannot rest upon a once-upon-a-time event of repentance. The posture and practice of repentance is not a single hurdle to clear at the start of our Christian life but is part of the pavement upon which we stride the whole way.

Realizing the deficiency in those approaches puts to us the question: are we genuinely searching ourselves to turn away from sin? Very few people explicitly and purposefully adopt a mindset of presumption upon their church membership to excuse a need for personal repentance. I would be shocked to my core if I heard a member in my congregation outright say something like, "It's perfectly fine for me to go through the motions of church without throwing my heart into a relationship with God." Still, is it possible that we unconsciously sink into that sort of mindset? One line of reasoning goes something like "I'm at church every Sunday, I'm in a Bible study, I help with practical aspects of church life *more* than loads of other people, I come to Wednesday prayer, so if I'm doing all that, how could I be trapped in sin and need to repent?" This rationale might hold up. It might also be the case we think this way because we have accidentally slipped into complacency in the Christian life.

---

11 For more on the blessing of church membership, see Jonathan Landry Cruse, *Church Membership* (Blessings of the Faith; P&R, 2024) or Harrison Perkins, *A Student's Guide to Living out Reformed Theology* (Track; Christian Focus, 2024), 67-75.

The simple takeaway is that we always need to be searching ourselves in order to repent. As John the Baptist announced, "Bear fruits in keeping with repentance." Even in this exhortation, the need for plural *fruits* that accord with repentance points beyond a one-time act toward an ongoing repetitive action.[12] We should not rest ourselves in mere broad confession of our need to repent. General repentance of that sort certainly has its rightful place, namely, as an admission that we are never able to comprehend our sinfulness or catalogue our sins sufficiently. A proper disposition of general repentance should foster—rather than replace—the practice of specific repentance. We must search ourselves to turn away from our sins. After all, we come to Christ to be freed of our sins. Let us keep fleeing to Him to be increasingly rid of our sin and increasingly full of the godliness that Christ would grant us by the power of the Spirit.

In this way, repentance is a great benefit of Christ. The purpose of searching ourselves is not that we would run without ceasing on the wheel of guilt. Rather, we want to cherish all the ways that Christ has showered grace upon us. We want to experience new levels of freedom from that which has shackled our hearts in the misery of sin. Our efforts at searching ourselves for repentance are not ways to merit God's favor. They are ways to *see* how God has already given us His favor in forgiving us of those sins. Repentance is a saving grace. It is an experience of the Lord's love. It is a taste of freedom given to us in Christ. Thus, our repentance must be real and an essential part of our life in the church.

Ongoing Repentance

Why is the effort to maintain an ongoing repentance so valuable? We have landed heavily on how God's grace is

---

12 Bock, *Luke*, 1:304.

freely given to us in Christ. Why then is repentance worth pursuing as a particular sort of experience of His love? What good is there in the type of self-conscious pursuit that we have commended in the preceding sections? What deeper motivation do we have for chasing this sort of ongoing repentance?

Good in Itself

Sanctification, that is our growth in godliness, is good in itself. We might too often mistakenly come to believe that growing in holiness is something that we *have* to do, forgetting that it is a blessing to be freed from the "old self" (Eph. 4:20-24; Rom. 6:6). We can think that sanctification is like taking out the trash: it has to be done, but it's an effort that itself is not rewarding. We need a deeper and stronger view of sanctification than that pessimistic take. After all, our growth in godliness is about Christ working in us by the Spirit to give us a fuller life of freedom from that which makes us miserable.

Being like Christ is inherently good. We do not need any better or greater result from sanctification than being more in the image of God's Son. For that reason, people who cherish Christ long to be like Him. Those called by Christ's name, and baptized into His body, should hunger and thirst for righteousness because it is good. What a blessing to us that, by God's grace, we can grow in reflecting the goodness of our very good Savior.

We ought then to remember that our sanctification is a gift from God for our good. Westminster Shorter Catechism 32 asks, "What *benefits* do they that are effectually called partake of in this life?", and answers that we receive "justification, adoption, and *sanctification*, and the several *benefits* which in this life do either accompany or flow from them." The emphasis is at least partly on how sanctification is a benefit to us. It comes to us from Christ as those who are in Christ receiving the blessings of His grace. We ought then to trust that the summons to pursue sanctification, which, according to Westminster Shorter Catechism 35, is a work of God's free grace, is not meant to shackle us into some dour restrictiveness. It means to show us the way out of the lingering factors of this life that make us miserable and dishonor God.

Good for Motivation

We should see now even more why our first chapter argued that the best pastoral approach to urging God's people toward repentance ought *not to begin* with the threats of hell. Christ's sheep often need help redirecting their lives. Pastors are called to feed those sheep, not to terrify them (John 21:15-19). The summons to repent of sin ought to lead with showing the sheep what rich blessings awaits in the green pastures of godliness so that they would *want* to leave the swamp marshes of sin. God has announced a gospel of freedom in Christ, so we ought to follow the biblical pattern of first calling His people back to that freedom (Gal. 5:1-15).

This priority of sanctification's goodness puts the pastoral use of warnings in better context. Should we not remember repentance is evidence of God's grace (2 Tim. 2:25)? Truly, we must repent because God's wrath is coming upon godlessness, as John the Baptist proclaimed: "You brood of vipers! Who warned you to flee from the wrath to come?… Even now the axe is laid to the root of the trees. Every tree therefore that does not bear good fruit is cut down and thrown into the fire" (Luke 3:7, 9). The truth of God's judgment upon sin cannot be absent from our message.

Are those threats the primary method for furthering God's people in their walk of sanctification? Once someone has come to Christ and professed faith in Him, should we keep threatening them with judgment as the way to help them grow in godliness? A sheep of Christ, who is steadily walking the straight and narrow path but with an occasional backward glimpse at his former life, needs his head nudged forward again to see the beauty of the field ahead of him on the path. That sheep will run faster in the right direction on that narrow path by knowing the goodness that adorns its every step. God has said as much in telling us that, "There is no fear in love, but perfect love casts out fear. For fear has to do with punishment, and whoever fears has not been perfected in love" (1 John 4:18). The goodness of Christ and the prospect of knowing His blessing even more will attract His sheep down the path of repentance more than any threat that they are slipping from Christ's love. Our summons to repentance is also simply a summons to keep facing toward Christ. To repent is to keep walking toward Him as we happen to be walking away from our sin in the process. To have less of sin is to have more of Christ.

How do we implement those aspects of warning? Without using threats of judgment as the main tool for motivating the sheep who are trying their best to go the right direction, we sadly have to acknowledge that sometimes members of our churches do turn around to walk the other direction entirely. Someone who professes faith in Christ can stumble and need gracious help to keep in step with the Spirit (Gal. 5:22-26). At times, however, someone can entrench themselves so thoroughly and impenitently in his or her sin that we can no longer believe that profession of faith. When we see a person nearing that point, we have to lean upon John the Baptist's announcement that the trees which do not bear proper fruit are fit to be chopped and burned (Luke 3:9). These warnings, though not suitable to keep sheep going in the right direction, are at times exactly what a sheep who has started walking in the wrong direction needs to hear.

The somber use of these warning shows us how serious they are. Although these threats are not empty, sheep who are believing and repenting should not be continually frightened as though they are in danger of being cut off from the Lord. The warnings are not exactly about not bearing *enough* fruit in keeping with repentance but about being the sort of tree that bears fruit. We want to be trees bearing fruits in keeping with repentance because it indicates God's work within us. When some start to bear fruit that is holistically not in accord with the posture and practice of repentance, then we have to help them see how that other sort of fruit indicates something rotten is at work in their hearts in a frightening way. It is not that repentance itself saves us, nor that our good works turn away God's wrath. It is that those in whom God has worked bear this sort of fruit that accords with repentance. Those whom God has called to faith in Christ learn to hate their sin, which means that those who have not turned from their sin have not trusted in the Savior.

A good diagnostic question is then: Do you *love* your sin? Do you *love* the unrighteous deeds you commit in thought, word, and action? If you strive after ungodly things, then you must know that God's wrath is coming and will rain down upon those who have committed ungodliness. By God's grace, however, you could repent and turn away from your love for sin.

The purpose of this diagnostic question is not to ask if you *do* sin. We all sin. Christians slip into sin of various kinds all the time. The value in asking if we *love* our sin is to pinpoint whether we prefer that sin over what Christ would have for us. If we *love* our sin and wish that we could indulge it, resisting it only because we think God will do bad things to us if we do not, then we clearly do not understand God's goodness and sin's vileness. We need to align with Paul's struggle in the Christian life: "For I do not understand my own actions. For I do not do what I want, but I do the very thing I hate" (Rom. 7:15). The penitent Christian, even as he or she sins, will have some level of hate for that sin, knowing that God's moral law is ultimately better for us.

Now, this part is crucial: we do not turn away from sin by turning simply to morality—we turn to Jesus Christ. The first motion in the repentant life must be turning to Jesus. We do not turn away from sin to find Jesus, but we flee to Jesus to be rid of our sin. As we have continually considered from Westminster Shorter Catechism 87, repentance is turning *unto God* because we have an apprehension of His mercy *in Christ*. Colquhoun marks a danger in thinking that Christ will not receive us until we have attained sufficient repentance, explaining that those who do not understand how repentance fits within the covenant of grace "dare not attempt coming to the gracious Redeemer till they are first satisfied that their repentance is of the *true* kind, until they can bring it as a price in their hand to procure their welcome." When we make adequate repentance a condition of coming to Christ, we turn it into a bargaining chip for why He should accept us. Hence, Colquhoun exhorts us that, "Instead of this, they ought without a moment's delay to come to Christ *for* true repentance." Christ will give us true repentance as we seek Him, so we should not turn our repentance into something we do to be worthy of forgiveness.[13] Just as you do not wash up before you shower, so too you do not try

13 Colquhoun, *Repentance*, 3–4 (italics original).

to get better to go to Christ. As one hymn expresses it, "if you tarry 'til you're better, you will never come at all."[14] We shower to get clean. We go to Christ to be made better.

In this way, sanctification is built on the gospel premise of justification. Christ credits His perfect record to you by faith and forgives all your sin. His merits cover even the imperfection of your works, but that is why we pursue those fruits in keeping with repentance as the tenor of the Christian life. Repentance is not the foundation. Christ and faith in Him are the foundation. Christ is the root and the tree, we are the branches connected thereunto, and our efforts to turn away from sin and race after holiness spring forth from being joined to Christ (John 15:1-17).

We must pursue ongoing repentance because it is the flavor of life with Christ. It is the melody of the Christian life. Thus, this race away from sin is simply the race toward our Savior who died to rescue us from sin in penalty and power, and who waits to say "Well done good and faithful servant" to all who turn to Him in true faith.

Conclusion

The beautiful thing about repentance as a staple feature of the Christian walk is that it highlights how Christ remains with us all our life long. Even though we are never fully rid of sin, even though we need to keep pursuing new repentance to obtain new sanctification, our deficiency means that we are also never rid of Christ. He walks continually with us through it all. So, as we pray and strive to bear fruits in keeping with repentance, we know that Christ is our loving gardener, tending His vine to nourish us.

---

14 Joseph Hart, "Come, Ye Sinners, Poor and Wretched," *Trinity Psalter Hymnal*, 400. Thanks to Jonathan Cruse for alerting me to these lyrics.

CONCLUSION

This book aimed to help Christ's people recover the posture and practice of repentance in a joyful way. The purpose has been to encourage you concerning what blessings reside in the vigorous pursuit of repentance as an ordinary part of the Christian life. Our final reflections here ought to bring home the benefits of this approach to our walk with Christ.

For those with tender consciences, you may read that phrase "the vigorous pursuit of repentance" and be overwhelmed with what *vigorous* might entail. How can we ever be vigorous enough in turning away from our sin? Well, I hope you might hear more clearly that repentance should be an *ordinary* part of the Christian life. God is not asking you for astounding feats of repentance so that you measure up at special intervals. Repentance is a blessing from Christ as He wants to lead you away from sin and its misery. It is meant to be a piece of the simple rhythm of our walk with Christ. My tender-hearted brother or sister, whether in your moment of strength or struggle, know that as you walk forward in the Christian life fueled by faith and wanting to be rid of your sin, Jesus is well pleased with you.

This point ought to be of comfort to those readers who worry that their repentance is not good enough to pass muster. We might easily worry that our repentance lacks certain qualities or sufficient quantity to appease God.[1] If the purpose of our repentance was to appease God, that worry would be valid. As we have explored though, repentance is not a prerequisite condition for God to accept us. It is the gift that comes from Christ to those whom He has bought as His own through the shedding of His blood, and whom He has made blameless before the presence of God's glory—so much so that we should have great joy as Christ presents us before the divine throne (Jude 24-25). The primary question is not: Is my repentance good enough. The primary question is: Is my Savior good enough? Of course, He is.

For those with stubborn consciences, you may read the phrase that repentance is "an ordinary part of the Christian life" and feel content that you are just fine. In my experience, however, those who have said to me, "I feel like I'm exactly where I need to be in my walk with God," have always been the ones for whom I was most concerned if they even knew the true God. We cannot let ourselves reach that place of hardness. For you, the emphasis may need to fall on *vigorous* pursuit. Indeed, repentance should be an ongoing feature of our lives as Christians. My stubborn-hearted brother or sister, I hope you might remember that He chose His people in grace with the purpose "that we should *be holy* and blameless before him" (Eph. 1:4). God does care deeply about holiness.

That this book might be read differently from those two competing perspectives marks our need for balance concerning how repentance fits into our lives. We all need to

---

1 Thanks to R. Scott Clark for flagging this concern as a point to address.

remember that complacency is not our friend. Since readers might interpret that point in different ways, our closing thoughts best serve us by considering what this truth means in more detail.

Perhaps, the most fitting metaphor is water. Water becomes stagnant when it sits still for too long. When there is no activity in the water, it ruins. We can apply the metaphor two ways. First, for my stubborn-hearted reader, movement is required to avoid stagnation. You have to go somewhere and have some activity. Seek the Lord that repentance might be a deeper concern in your life. Second, for my tender-hearted reader, might you see that you do not need to be the torrent of Niagara Falls to avoid stagnation. The steady but soft trickle of a babbling brook often provides some of the freshest water. Although movement is required to avoid stagnation, it need not be a movement that empties our entire reservoir. Rest in the Lord as He moves you evenly along the path of this life, helping you to believe and to repent better each day as He wills.

The lingering problem to address might be, what if I—to the best that I understand myself—have repented but now I still do not *feel* that relief that should accompany repentance? I used to live in Britain, and all the houses in which we lived there had radiators as the heating system. The issue with radiators is, even when you turn the heat on, it can take a really long time for that heat to makes its way into all the water filling those radiators. The heat is coming. Nevertheless, it does not always come instantly. That was especially true if that water had been sitting cold a long time.

Even when we repent, it does not mean the consolation will come in one instant. That is especially true if we have been "sitting cold" in impenitence for a long time. The colder that we have been, the longer it might take to feel warmed by the power of Christ as we repent. So, if we have been deeply entrenched in sin for some time, the comfort of God's approval may (metaphorically!) have some distance to travel before it turns the water of our souls warm again.

Westminster Larger Catechism 175 raises this same concern about what to do if someone does not feel the comfort and help that they should in receiving the Lord's Supper. The advice there is that "if they find no present benefit, more exactly review their preparation to and carriage at the sacrament" so that if they find themselves approved in conscience and before God "they are to wait for the fruit of it in due time" or to humble themselves if they have failed. The same practice can apply to our repentance. Christ is dependable. He will provide His comfort in due time to every repentant sinner who comes to Him for grace.

In all these thoughts, we must never abandon this base point that repentance brings us back to Jesus. We come to Him to be rid of our sins. We turn away from our sins as we see the misery they inflict. As we commit to the posture and practice of repentance, we learn how to say to Christ, "You make known to me the path of life; in your presence there is fullness of joy; at your right hand are pleasures forevermore" (Ps. 16:11).